Spiritual Ice Breakers

A path to God-After Spiritual Bondage

Gloria Murphy

ISBN 978-1-64191-607-3 (paperback)
ISBN 978-1-64191-608-0 (digital)

Christian Faith Publishing, Inc.
832 Park Avenue
Meadville, PA 16335
www.christianfaithpublishing.com

Cover photo taken by Martin Capek. The title is Earth Apocalypse in the Fire and Ice Lightning.

Extracts used with permission from the booklet "The Facts on the Occult" by John Ankerberg and John Weldon.

Printed in the United States of America

DEDICATION

I dedicate this book to God, my Father who is behind
every single word and who I owe my life to.

I also like to thank my husband who has devoted as
much time as I have to completing this book.

To my daughter who spent many a long night over distances afar
and close, supporting me in finding my voice and getting every
word printed, through all the emotion and reflections – we did it!

To my Son who helped me with lots of support and confirmations.

And last but not least I dedicate this book to Margaret Bell
who confirmed to me that this book had to be written.

SPECIAL THANK YOU to

Rev. Dr. Alistair P. Petrie. Executive Director
of Partnership Ministries

For reading my manuscript and all the Godly encouragement given

Randie S. Long, Lawyer and Mediator for Merrill, Long
and Company, for your time and professional help.

CONTENTS

Part 3: Early Days as a Christian

Part 4: God and Mike's Proposal

INTRODUCTION

I was led to write this book by God Himself to help people make better decisions in their spiritual lives. We are far more spiritual than we are physical beings. Many people struggle to find a sense of belonging within them, so they go looking for things that they think will fulfill the emptiness within. We are so much more than a physical form; we all long for a spiritual connection within, with our creator who is God. So what are you looking for? This relates to all people whether Christian or not.

What I think is important in this life is for people to get connected deeply within themselves, connected to God, to let their spirit and their soul be guided by the Holy Spirit rather than anything else. If you connect with the wrong source, it is like connecting with the wrong radio station; you can be misguided and sabotage your own life.

I lived the first half of my life tapped into the wrong station, and eventually my life degenerated into a chaotic hell. At this point, I was so low and so taken over by the wrong spiritual powers that there wasn't much left of the real me anymore. Through a series of life-changing events, God came into my life in miraculous ways. My transformation is the content of this book both before my transformation and after. I am blessed to be able to share the events of my life with you, for it is by the grace of God that I am here now to share my journey.

Hi. My name is Gloria, from the Latin word meaning glory and great bearer of truth. I am a bearer of great news. God and Jesus delivered me from a life of occult practices, which were embedded in my family line for decades. After my deliverance, I have been asked time and again to relay my testimony and the circumstances that brought me before our God. God wants His people to be aware and mindful of the ways of demonic practices, which are often accepted by Christians. In all that we do, being aware and always focused on God and Christ Jesus, we will be able to transcend our own lives and help those around us see the light. (You and I could be a living example of the embodiment of Christ, so let us be the light and guide for those who are searching for truth.)

I give to you through Jesus Christ my testimony and dedication, which I pray will help you be enlightened and aware of the powers that surround us today. I firmly believe that we are now in a revelation period of time where the chaff will be separated from the wheat. It has never been a more important time to be clean before God and pure in your thoughts and actions.

It is dangerous to be meddling with anything to do with the occult. Nobody should meddle in the supernatural, witchcraft, or any other type of activity, as doing so encourages more of the same in your life. I was born into the supernatural at birth and have come through it by the grace of God. I write this book to enlighten people on the powers that exist in this world, both good and evil. There are two choices in this world today—either heaven or hell. There is no middle road, so it is important to make the right choice.

PART 1

The Dark Side

CHAPTER 1

The Dark Side

I was born December 9, 1938 in Surrey, England. I am the eldest child in my family, the only girl, followed by three brothers. My father drank for as long as I can remember, and he was mentally and sometimes physically abusive. I should have been a boy in my father's eyes; he was never comfortable with me. My mother stayed home and raised us. I know now that she was involved with the occult and spiritualism as well as spiritual healing. Both my mother and my grandmother had received gifts in these areas. Another word would be that they were mediums. They were into the occult, which is the knowledge and study of the supernatural or magical forces. Growing up with my mother and my grandmother, with whom I was very close, I accepted these occult practices as normal and part of life. I know now that these practices are not permissible by God. But now I am getting ahead of myself. I wasn't a Christian yet, and while I grew up in the world of spiritualism, occult, and mediums, which was a life all too familiar to me, my biggest transformation would not happen until some fifty years later when I gave my life to God.

I had no idea that I would inherit dark spirits. I did not know that this "spiritual" thing we all shared had been in the family for generations, flowing from the female line. I am the eldest and only girl, my daughter is the eldest and only girl, my mother eldest and only girl, and so on. Furthermore, somewhere along the family line, some female in my family must have cursed God and been heavily into the occult. God broke that curse when he delivered me and broke the line, so my daughter also was set free—free to make her own choices, the same for my son. It was the first time I was aware that God had intervened in my life, but I wasn't aware of this happening nor did I get confirmation of it until after I was delivered.

The spirits that used me throughout my life convinced me that my life was "special," so I felt special and believed this to be true. Why would I not believe them? They spoke to me from the time I was a child. Later, there would be more of them inside of me and far less of me. Throughout my whole life, the spirits that used me kept growing stronger and stronger.

Right from an early age, I kept to myself. I read books to do with the supernatural such as *Life After Death,* and I was taken to a spiritualist church to see healings by the laying on of hands by a prophet. I even watched this prophet use instruments and cut people with them and put things in their mouths. I watched amazed as blood flowed and was stopped.

I was witnessing spiritual healings. These people would be healed of one thing, but what bad spirits were they accepting into their bodies in return? These practices are quite common in occultism where spirits are transferred through body fluids, food, and even through telepathic practices. In all cases, if the participant is willing, spirits can enter you even if you are simply ignorant of such practices. That is why it is so important to be aware of these things so that you are not a receptor to darkness coming into your life.

As a human being, you are never really free until God frees you through Christ. I have come to learn that if you believe in your full freedom in Christ Jesus, then evil cannot defeat you but can only harass you because you are in Christ Jesus (Romans 8:1).

I had voices that talked to me all of the time. They guarded me (Gloria), always kept me safe, and made me feel secure and special. These spirits were so close to me I really didn't need people.

Remember I was just a young child aged five years old onwards. Being with these spirits was much better than being with my family where my father physically and psychologically abused me (not sexually). I was treated differently from the three boys, and I hated it. I could do nothing right. My mother told me, "Your father loves you." This only warped my impression of love. I would think to myself, how on earth does he love me? He was so cruel to me most of the time. But I always had my voices, which helped to fill the void.

At school, the voices would give me answers to questions, especially in math. I would take a problem in mathematics and have the right answer. I could never show the teacher how I got all my answers right because my spirits told me the answers. I loved art and was good at it. I received good marks in school, sometimes coming first in the class (with the help of the spirits within me). My father would say, "How much did you cheat?" Thinking about it after, I guess I did cheat because my voices helped me. They were more real to me than people themselves. My voices taught me how to leave my body at will. I found it very easy to read people's minds, and I always knew what they were thinking.

I was overly sensitive and had a poor self-image, but my voices would rally around me and boost me up. I learned to not talk about them or all the things I saw in the spiritual realms. They were always telling me that I was different and very special. Even though people thought I was a nobody, my spirit friends were training me to be a somebody, and they told me that people would regret hurting me. This helped to inflate my ego and give me much confidence, which I desperately needed.

Around the age of ten, things started to change for me and not for the better. My father hated me even more passionately, and I didn't know why. To stop the hurt and pain so that I could survive these circumstances I lived in, I had a plan and started to unlove my father and replace love with hate. I would talk over my plan with my spirit friends, and they agreed with me, that separation was the answer to my suffering. After that, I started to dissociate myself from my parents, and I was determined to do better than just survive. It worked.

This separation I experienced within myself is key to the beginning of demise for any person whether they are Christian or not. Once we become separated from ourselves, it is very easy for anything to take over. Some people experience being taken over by their ego, and they give all of themselves over to a crude version of themselves, acting from emotion and childish desires. Separation is perhaps the one key factor that ignites many physiological problems in people. Even as a Christian, if you are not fully connected to yourself and fully in tune with who you are, you can more easily experience hardship in your walk with Christ and be derailed or enticed away from Christ. A strong connection to self is key to a strong and solid walk with Christ.

Once I separated from my family and myself, I became defiant and a whole lot of other things. Being hit by my father didn't hurt as much because I learned to leave my body, and I would come back when he was done. I still had a problem with the verbal abuse and the "cat and mouse game" my father would play against me. My nerves were very bad, and I lived with a lot of stress. I succeeded at whatever I put my mind to. I was going to show my father I was nothing like him. My spiritual friends agreed with me and always filled the void I had deep in my soul.

I left school and could not wait to leave home. I was married at eighteen, and my husband was twenty-one. I moved to Stevenage and was interviewed for a job with Lloyds Bank and passed with flying colors with the help of my spirit friends. The job at Lloyds for which I was evaluated on required five years of previous experience, and I was able to pick up the skills I needed in two months, so the position was mine. Other girls there said I must have lied about having no previous experience just to make myself look more knowledgeable than I was. I just had my spirit friends who never left me.

I had a baby at twenty-three years old, a little girl I named Darice. My spirit friends told me to name her Darice. The meaning of my daughter's name is Persian meaning princess or queenly. What had she been born into? The same things as myself? As a family, we decided to immigrate to Canada two years later. My emotions were off the wall. There were a lot of strange things happening to me, so much so that I became physically and mentally disturbed. I didn't tell anyone, I just tried to keep going, trying to look good. I had a couple of nervous breakdowns within a few years of arriving in Canada, and I was already seeing a psychiatrist before my breakdowns. My husband didn't have a clue that anything was wrong with me.

My husband didn't drink, he had a job, and he saved money. He was nothing like my father, that's why I married him. Later my husband became extremely tight with money and very controlling and verbally abusive like my father. But I still had my spirit friends, whom my husband knew nothing about. I never asked my husband how I looked to him, even though I knew there was something wrong with me. I had these spirit things inside of me, and they were affecting my behavior, my mind, and my body.

We came to Canada and settled in London, Ontario. I figured I had left all my bad memories from my past behind and that I would have a new start. Guess what, my spirit friends came with me. I had left my parents and brothers behind. I applied for and obtained a good job. I didn't write or phone back to UK. I figured it was great that I was in Canada and family was back in UK, a long way away. I felt freedom for the first time in years, but it was short-lived.

CHAPTER 2

Effects of Spiritual Training

One Christmas, I bought my husband Tarot cards, and I ended up being the one using them. I could also read Runes. Friends would come to me for readings. It was so natural for me to work with anything spiritual. But still my mind was giving me problems; I was tormented from the inside out. The spirits in me played with me and stretched me to see if I would snap, yet I still saw them as my friends. I was so isolated at this point and entrapped. They had replaced everything meaningful in my life. I was reading New Age books and buying semiprecious stones, including crystals. My spirit friends were teaching me how to use these spiritual tools, and they said they would make me grow in wisdom. I was having strong visions and profound dreams. My spirit friends were putting me through spiritual training in these dreams. Battles were fought in gladiator arenas, I was being conditioned. I was fighting demons and winning. An angel of light was always at my side. Piece by piece, I won all of my Roman armor, including a cloak. It was a cloak similar to what the Romans would wear with a large clasp fastening on one side. I had the belt, breastplate, shield, sword, and helmet to match.

Imagine how I felt when as a Christian I saw and read in the Bible about the whole armor of God in Ephesians 6:10–17. It states that the whole armor of God includes *all* the Roman armor I had earned. I realized later that the devil is such a copycat of God's doings. I know now that God created all of these things first, and the devil cannot create anything other than chaos. At the time I became a Christian, I found the similarities between the dark and light side confusing. Under the devil, there are demons and angels of light all working on the same side. When I fought my battles in my Roman armor in my dreams, I would be fighting demons and then rescued by angels of light. But both of them were working for the devil. I found this very confusing after my deliverance, to see angels of light on the dark side, you would think angels of light belonged to God, not so. The devil will do anything to get you to believe in his powers and getting you to worship him. Yet he can only do it by copying God's powers. When I became connected to the Holy Spirit within me, I could then discern the difference between the angels of light under the devil and the true angels of God.

In one vision, I know that I met Lucifer (satan). At the time, I believed I was seeing an agent of God. I entered a palace where everything was very stark, clean, and shiny white. I saw many angels of light in the room glowing brilliantly, paying homage to this heavenly being who entered the room. One of the angels introduced me through telepathy to him. This being had so much charisma I was drawn to him. He wasn't very tall; he was beautiful and shone radiantly and wore a white suit. He did not speak a word to me, yet I knew he was telling me that I was on the right path. I was in awe, and I remembered this dream for many years it literally melted me inside every time I thought of it. When I was delivered, this vision came back to me, and I realized it was satan. Once all the falseness and artificial realities were cleaned up from my soul, I could see the truth very clearly. I suffered greatly as a young woman with mental conditions, which touched on extreme anxiety, fear, loss of a sense of myself, and depression. In my late twenties, I was so disturbed that I went to my family doctor for help. After an evaluation, he admitted me to a psychiatric hospital where I stayed for about six weeks. It was there that I met my psychiatrist and a social psychiatric worker, Ms. Reed. In the psychiatric ward of this hospital, I had a couple of bad experiences. The first thing my new doctor did was take me off all medication. A medical team watched me closely, and they thought I had more than one personality. Then they thought I had schizophrenia. At one point, the doctors talked about giving me shock treatments.

After I was released from hospital, the medical team informed me of their strategy to get to the root of my problem. They were determined to figure out a plan to break the part of me that I was masquerading so I could start to heal. It was extremely important to shatter my false show of pretense and get to the root of my anxieties. This team saw that I was not who I appeared to be. So, their plan of attack was for me to see the psychiatrist at five thirty in the morning, without showering, eating or dressing first. I would show up in my pajamas and housecoat to get my therapy. This was effective.

I would see my doctor for an hour or two in a darkened office. He would sit at an angle, never behind a desk, never full frontal, so I could only ever see half of him. After these sessions, I felt too sick to eat breakfast. Then after breakfast, I would go into group therapy with fifteen other people, of which my social psychiatric worker was in charge. When I came out of that, I couldn't eat lunch; in fact, I felt sick to my stomach. At this point in the day, I felt so sick, uncomfortable, and defenseless that I didn't want to speak to anybody. The result was that my therapist was gradually penetrating my hard security walls. Essentially, they were trying to get me to reconnect with the real me, which was so badly fragmented at that time I was barely myself anymore. Initially, they could not figure out what was wrong with me, and that was because I hid myself so well, even though that was not my conscious intention. I was doing what I was told to do by the spirits inside of me.

There was an incident in the hospital that explains how much my spirits had control of my life and how much they protected me as their host. I was a week or two into my therapy in the psychiatric ward, and I noticed that there were three priests and five nuns in the same ward as I was as patients! I found this very strange. I wondered what they were doing in a place like this. *What kind of place is this?* It actually made me feel better to know that if they need psychiatric help, then there was nothing wrong with me needing the same kind of help. I was in a semiprivate room, which I shared with another patient. Right from the start, she was asking me why I was there and what was wrong with me. I felt uncomfortable, but I just ignored her. She then told me in no uncertain terms that she didn't think I should be there and that I was taking a bed away from someone who really needed it. She accused me of pretending to be sick. Little remarks here and there from her really started to irritate me. I didn't like hearing again and again, "You really shouldn't be here," it was what I heard all my life. Then one day, she came into the room that we shared, but with her was another woman who was also hospitalized, and they both closed the door behind them. I was sitting on my bed, and I was wondering why they did this. They started to tell me again how I shouldn't be there. I knew something was rising up inside of me that wasn't me.

What was in me attacked them verbally. Next thing I knew, an alarm bell rang, and nurses came running in. I was yelling and screaming, saying, "Get those two out of my room!" I told the nurses that I did not want them to let those women back in my room again. I then saw another psychiatrist, and he asked if I wanted to be in a "padded" room. He was trying to be nice, and he knew how drastically I had exploded. I told him I was fine, so they put me in a private room with a nurse watching me for the next twenty-four hours.

That night, my spirits tormented the nurse who was on patient watch in the room with me. They were saying to her, "You are scared, aren't you?" I could tell by the atmosphere in the room that my spirits were in control. I could see it happening in front of me, and I was powerless to control what was coming out of my mouth. They taunted her through me. When I think back on this incident today, I remember how empty I felt at the time. I really didn't care what she felt or what she had gone through that night. The next day, I was put in another room for the duration of my stay. During my time there, I was once again asked what I thought about receiving electric shock treatments. I was dead against it because I felt my brain was already messed up enough. I was allowed to go home on the week-ends, and eventually I was released. In the end, the psychiatrist team that worked with me determined that I was "chronically neurotic."

After I was released from the hospital, I had to continue seeing the psychiatrist five days a week for the next eight years. I just knew that if I had spoken in any length about my spirit friends, I would have been admitted into a mental hospital, which was something neither I nor my spirit friends wanted. I also knew that I wasn't crazy because I was able to discern and reason with my voices, and together we discussed what to tell the doctors and what not to tell them. I often wondered afterwards about the number of people who are in mental hospitals who really should not be there because their condition is based on being possessed by spirits and not based on a mental disorder. After my treatments, I was released, and my life continued as "normal."

I still never spoke to my doctors about my spirit friends; in fact, I spoke to *no one* about them. They made it very clear to me to *not* talk to other people about them. Somewhere in those eight years, my husband and I decided to have another child, and my son was born. I was feeling much better and fairly stable after eight years of therapy. I was doing well in my job and had some close friends and a beautiful home. As a family, it was decided that we should go back and visit our families in UK with my husband, daughter, and son. My son was only eighteen months old when we all went back to England. My demon friends told me not to go back to UK. My husband and my doctors all felt I would be fine to go back. I went back thinking I was okay.

Miss Reed, who was my social psychiatric worker at the time, told me that she was going to be in Ireland at the same time I would be England. She gave me her contact number and encouraged me to call her at any time if I felt I needed it. While I was in England, I was a mess. There were too many memories. I almost overdosed on my prescription medication because I was trying desperately to appear normal. Seeing my father and mother being so nice to me made me feel sick. All the old hurts, pains, and memories came flooding back to me. I realized with great sadness and overwhelming depression that I was not really well at all. I couldn't take it. Everyone in UK that we visited seemed so fake to me. I couldn't get past the past. I thought I had dealt with it all, but in reality, I had simply buried it. It all seemed so pretentious to me, the way my family was acting and the way I was with myself.

I never called Miss Reed. I tore her number up so I would not be able to call her. My voices were silent. I was left alone in my misery and struggling every day to manage all the mixed feelings and emotions I was feeling. It was not a good time. During the last few days in England, I planned my escape. I would go back to Canada and do away with myself. It seemed the best and most logical thing to do after being such a failure in my own life. Once I made up my mind about what I was going to do, I felt much better. I planned my final days well. Shortly after returning from England, I cleaned the house, wrote my suicide note, took capsules of the strongest medication I had, and went to sleep.

When I woke up, I was in the hospital for a couple of weeks and under observation as needed after that. The doctors released me fairly quickly because I was doing so well. I felt amazing and really free. It seemed to not make sense after trying to commit suicide that I should feel as good as I did. After living my daily life in complete turmoil and stress for the last several years, I finally felt a huge release, and was actually really happy to be alive. When I returned to work after a five-week absence, I asked my boss to relieve me of my managerial role, and I wanted to be just one of the girls. They allowed me to come back in a less stressful position. As a result, I was able to carry on. Unfortunately, my happiness didn't last long.

What came out of my therapy was that the relationship I had with my mother and my father was very dysfunctional. I was shocked to learn how much I hated my father. This also meant that I had serious trust issues with men. Finally admitting my feelings about my family released a whole chain of emotions that I would have to work through for the next twenty years of my life. As my therapy progressed, I was more able to set healthy boundaries in my relationships and find a sense of myself, albeit slowly.

Increasingly, I could not ignore the fact that things were not good between my husband and me. As I became stronger within myself, problems started to arise between us concerning power and control issues. When I was very disturbed, I was not myself and was quite dependent and passive. Now that I was finding myself, I was discovering that I was actually strong-willed and far from passive. My husband had a hard time adapting to the new me, and we often had conflicts. I also had a lot of anger issues, which unfortunately played out in destructive ways. Meanwhile, what was inside of me was possessive of my time and me. My spirits and I were becoming more and more like one. With my attachments to the spirit world, how could I have a good marriage? The spirits were not going to share me with anybody.

After returning from England, my therapist was teaching me how to stand up for myself where my husband was concerned. I remember one incident where there was a very good friend of mine who was leaving Canada Trust and there was a farewell party after work. My husband had been invited, and he said he would not go and that I was not to go either. I decided to go anyway since I was feeling confident after my talk with Ms. Reed. I went to the party after work with my friends. I was having a great time and wanted to stay later, so I called my husband, and I asked him if I could stay (gosh! what a stupid thing to say, Gloria). My husband told me to get home right away and then put the phone down. When he did that, I figured I was in trouble anyway, so I decided to stay for as long as I wanted. My rebellious side was coming out.

My friend drove me home, and I asked her to wait outside for me because I thought that I might be locked out. Surprisingly, my key went into the lock, and I waved good-bye to her and went into the house. There was a note on the table telling me I needn't bother going upstairs to our bedroom and that I wasn't good enough to sleep in the same room with him. I then walked to the bottom of the stairs, and there was my nightdress at the bottom of the stairs. Something rose up inside of me.

I went upstairs, and I knew he was awake. We started to argue. I told him that I had a really good time, and that was why I was late. My husband told me I was acting like a child and that he was going to treat me like a child. He then told me that he was going to put me over his knee and give me a spanking for being disobedient. "No way," I said and then left the bedroom and went to the bathroom to brush my teeth. I picked up a drinking glass and threw it against the door of the bathroom as a warning for him to stay away. I could hear him coming, so I threw another glass against the door.

The two glasses had shattered all over the floor. He pushed the door open and walked in and promptly stepped on the broken glass. With blood everywhere and him cursing, I could not help but see this as funny because I felt he had asked for it. To get out of the bathroom, I had to walk all over that glass, but not one piece of glass cut me. After that, he wouldn't talk to me for ages. I got into my side of the bed, as I owned half the bed anyway, and we shared a silent cold sleep—ingredient for one unhappy marriage. I thought he was a bully. As more incidents like this one arose between us, I could see how it was going to be a battle to the end between my husband and me. I can hardly blame him for reacting strongly to the new me that was emerging. Unfortunately, I just knew that the new me was not the kind of wife he would want. He was not able to change me.

Who was going to help me? Who was going to rescue me? How much more pain could my physical body stand? I didn't know it at the time, but I so needed God.

CHAPTER 3

Hell on Earth

U p until this point, the spirits in me had been somewhat dormant; however, they soon became active again. They were not going to let me go. I had a real sense that they owned me. When would I be free? There were times when I was like a walking zombie. I lived my life by the clock, like a robot. It was the only way I could function because the spirits kept harassing me. I used to sleep only three to four hours a night. They would kick me out of my body, and I would be living in a flat void. When this happened, I couldn't come back into my body until they allowed me to come back. I was scared sometimes to go to sleep because I thought they might prevent me from coming back into my body, forcing me to live in a hellish type of void. It was like being thrown out into outer space, but there were no stars; it was black as black. I could only go back into my body when they gave me permission. My spirits were using my body while I was in this void. I felt like I was being pulled apart, cell by cell. Even though I may have had only four hours sleep a night, I still had loads of energy by day. I was experiencing more and more out-of-body experiences as time went on.

My spirits were training me for battle. These battles were similar to the Roman gladiator battles I was having in my dreams. There were different levels I had to go through, which were becoming increasingly more difficult. I was aware of graduating through many different levels in the spiritual realm. It was similar to dungeons and dragons games. Sometimes my spirit could enter into the bodies of animals. One night, as part of my training by the spirits, I went into a body of a wild dog. It was living in and around the tombs in Egypt. In this particular incident, I saw through the eyes of a wild dog. I remember seeing a full moon. It was huge. I knew I was in a body that was not mine. I saw that I had a tail, and I was shocked to see that I had paws as well. One by one, I lifted my paws, taking in my new body. Then I began running all around the tombs. When I came back into my human body, I knew that I should not talk to my doctors, or anyone for that matter, about my out-of-body experiences.

Back to my first marriage. Things became more and more complicated. As I was growing rebellious and starting to define who I thought I was, problems in my marriage increased. My husband was extremely uncomfortable with the new me. I continued my psychiatric support during this time, and I was slowly getting stronger. I was very successful in my banking job, and at one point, I even made more money than my husband, which he was not comfortable with. As I started to grow and change, he became more controlling and angry. As I became stronger, the spirits inside of me also got stronger. However, I struggled with moments of paranoia and had panic attacks from time to time. For example, I was terrified that whenever my husband took the kids out, I had a phobia that they were all going to die. I would call the hospitals and the police to see if they were involved in an accident. I couldn't bear to be alone. When I was left on my own, I would hit my head against the wall and try and hurt myself so the pain I felt would mask the torment that was inside of me.

I was still having issues with my past and my dysfunctional family upbringing as well as trying to understand the meaning of the voices in my head. I was questioning everything. Spirits inside of me were controlling me. I was starting to come forward into my authentic self (whatever that means), and my husband thought he had me under control! What a laugh. But the spirits were controlling me even more and getting stronger the stronger I grew. What a mess. I still worked full time for the bank in a data communications department. At this time, there were so many things going on inside of me that I didn't understand. Meanwhile, on the outside, I looked pretty normal, but it took all of my energy to appear that way. I had my boss, my husband, my kids, and even my social psychiatric worker, Ms. Reed, all fooled. I deceived everybody. In fact, I had Ms. Reed convinced that she was making headway with me by letting her believe that I was improving. It was quite easy for me to know what people were thinking, so I knew how to get people to see me the way they wanted to see me. I realize now that I did this because I didn't want anyone to know that there was something definitely wrong with me. With voices in my head and spirits still guiding my life, I felt far from normal.

During these turbulent times, I was obsessed with watching happy families' going about their activities in stores, parks, malls, etc. I wanted to see how close they were, what they did together, and how they interacted with each other so I could learn to have a normal family life. What I most wanted in my life always seemed to evade me. My spirit friends effectively sabotaged my obsession to be part of a happy family, creating division between my husband and I, and disconnecting me from my kids. The spirits controlled me best if I was not connected to anyone, especially family. It tormented me that I was clearly not normal, and that normal family life evaded me. Admitting this truth made me feel a failure. I buried it within me, creating an even deep wedge between myself and my true desires.

CHAPTER 4

Scoop on Reincarnation

As part of my healing, I went one night to see Miss Reed with my husband. I wanted to start to make a real effort to have a better life and a better relationship with my husband. After seeing Ms. Reed for about eight years now, I decided it best for her to meet my husband. Halfway through our meeting, I suddenly wondered why I was even there. I didn't really want to spend another twenty years with my husband. I realized in that moment in her office that I had already given up on the marriage. I agreed with everything she suggested for us to do to make our marriage work better. I was so shocked at this revelation that I was not able to tell my doctor or my husband. In my mind, I sabotaged all the things that were suggested for us to do in our marriage. I said yes in all the right places, and three weeks later, I walked out on my marriage.

I was also at the same time seeing my best friend's husband on the side. My friend and I worked for the same company, and I would often bump into Fred, her husband. We were getting closer and closer over the next few weeks of our meetings when we both decided to leave our current marriages to be together. When I think of it now, he was a great vehicle for me to leave an unhappy marriage. My spirit friends were in total agreement with this. At the time, it didn't matter to me that I was leaving my marriage to be with my best friend's husband. I had a cold and calculating attitude about it. I needed to survive, and I felt I was worth more than the person I was with in my current marriage. Leaving my husband for another man was my attempt to continue my search for myself and reclaim who I was, even though I was still quite lost. (Think how sick is that?) I was finding my way. I was also searching and needed a change. How callous and calculating of *me*. There were times where people meant absolutely nothing to me. It was about *me* and them, my spirit friends.

I didn't think about my children. I knew one thing for sure at that time, and that was that I needed to get out of that marriage. I knew I had to do what I needed to do to survive, and I wouldn't have lasted much longer with my husband. Just to keep things straight, my first husband divorced me, January 1978. Fred and I married, June 9, 1978. Fred and I moved in together; we were soon divorced from our spouses, bought a house, and then married, taking my daughter and son with us. We tried to make a life together, but it was difficult in the early days of our marriage. Why wouldn't it be? I was so desperate to have a happy family with my second husband and my son and daughter there with us. The spirits were making sure I was aware of them more and being very active in my life at the same time.

My new husband and I went away after we were married for three days. I left my daughter in charge of babysitting. I came home and knew something was not right in the house. I challenged my daughter and found out that she had had her boyfriend over and that they had been drinking. I got all the children together in the kitchen and questioned them. My son, who has always been quite sensitive to spirits, said he saw a man's blue face floating all around me while I was questioning them. He told me what he saw, but I was so angry at the time trying to figure out what happened over the weekend that I snapped back at him, "So what!" And then he remained silent.

I sorted the incident out as best I could. There were loads of problems. That same night, I put my son to bed, and just my husband and I were together. I was so angry because this was our honeymoon, and I was having to deal with a delinquent daughter, who was supposed to take care of things while I was gone yet didn't. I went out to the garden, frustrated because it wasn't working; the marriage, the happy family with the kids, nothing was working out the way I expected. So, I sat down on the ground and gave up. Everything that I tried to do didn't work. I felt hopeless and defeated. I thought, *If this is living, what is the point?* I had left Fred in the kitchen. I must have stayed outside for two to three hours. I asked myself, where was my life going? I longed to be happy.

Voices were calling me from inside the house, saying, *Come here, come to us.* With my mind, I told the voices, *Get lost, I'm not interested in you.* Eventually, I decided to go into the house, and there was my husband still in the same chair in the same place as when I left hours earlier. He hadn't moved. He looked like he was sleeping. I said, "Fred, this is not funny. What is going on here?" Then he started to quote Shakespeare to me. Now this is a man who would not have been able to quote Shakespeare if you had paid him a million dollars. He was quoting from plays like the "Taming of the Shrew," "Merchant of Venice." I realized that the spirits were making sure I knew that Fred had been kicked out of his body. I knew it was spirits talking to me through him.

They talked through Fred for the next two and a half hours. They settled me down. They talked to me calmly. They answered all my questions about what would happen to my kids, my life, and me. They told me I was special. They could read my mind, so they knew that I was contemplating ending my life again. They said they had a special place for me and that they had special things they wanted me to do. They assured me that my children would be looked after. They said they really loved me and that they had loved me since I was born. They talked me out of my anger, and I was feeling much more hopeful about my life *again*!

It took Fred a while to come back to himself. While this was all going on, his spirit was up on the ceiling watching the whole event transpire beneath him in the kitchen. He was listening to himself speak Shakespeare, and when he came back into his body, he said that he had felt raped, dirty, and very unhappy. He was looking at me like I was a devil from hell with seven heads. Good start to a wonderful marriage? Not!

The spirits entered into my husband's body other times as well. One time, he was sitting at the kitchen table, and he wrote a letter not in his handwriting. My spirits said that it was from my grandmother. In the letter, it read, "I had to be obedient to my calling. I had to not obstruct my development in what was required of me. I was in good hands and must trust them more. My development with them would know no bounds." Fred wrote this with his eyes closed, and I even went under the table to look up and verify this. Amazingly, he wrote beautifully on lined paper, and it wasn't his handwriting. Again, when he came back to his body, he felt raped and dirty, and he was looking at me horrified, like I was responsible for it all. I was angry at his reaction to me. I felt that his complaints about being kicked out of his body where unfounded since I had to live with these spirits in my body my whole life.

It didn't faze me at all that he was kicked out of his body again because I had been kicked out of my body over and over again throughout my life. I was so deep in this spiritual mess that I couldn't even define what was normal anymore. Whenever I would wander away from them in my mind and not do what they wanted or not do it well, they did everything in their power to get me back on their track on their program.

When I wouldn't listen to them, they would enter Fred, and the fight would be on. Whenever I was disobedient, they would leave my body and enter into Fred and talk back to me through Fred. Things in our household were just getting worse. My daughter was into booze and drugs. In the end, she went to live with her father. I also had a couple of incidents with my daughter that were difficult to deal with at the time. It was almost as if she instinctively knew that I was going crazy. What was in me was trying to get my daughter into line. On top of dealing with all the spiritual drama going on in my life, I was also trying to deal with my daughter who was being a rebellious teenage, smoking pot, drinking, and doing her own thing. In the end, I had to let her go.

Fred and I were discussing new career options. I had a lot of pressure at work, and I was feeling a pull for me to leave the city where we lived. Fred was also feeling very strongly about leaving his job and moving on to something new. We decided to buy a store in a small town forty minutes outside of the city. When we found the store, it was perfect. It was a small grocery/convenience store with living quarters above, and it met all of our needs. We soon moved in. We did renovations, and our business grew. It seemed that once we made this move out of the city, out of our jobs, and into our new location, my life actually seemed to calm down. I was still very much in communication with my spirits. They approved of the move and the store in a good way. It must have been their idea. In every aspect, the new store was spot-on for what they wanted. I was being obedient to the calling in my life. The spirits were right in with us, they wanted us to buy the store, and everything went smoothly. We had my son and Fred's son living with us, and at first everything seemed to be going on really well.

Right from the beginning, the Native Indians that lived in the area among the three reserves started to come into the store, curious about the new owners. Native Indians very quickly made up 50 percent of our clientele. We did more renovations, and business became very good very quickly.

About four years into running the store together, Fred and I were finding it difficult to work together. I had my way of running things, and he had his way. So, we bought the garage next to the store, and he ran that business, while I looked after the store. I slowly started to realize that my husband also had a roaming eye for the ladies. One incident comes to mind. We had met a young couple. He was a trucker, and he and his wife, I now realize, were into the black arts. Fred thought they were the best people he had ever met, but not I. I was friendly but kept my distance. The wife and I had a falling out. We agreed to meet at the dome to sort it out without the men. The dome was what I was building on the ninety-seven-acre farm, directed by the spirits living in me.

As we walked over the land, she said to me that, "I know that I have fought you in previous lives and will continue to fight you in this life." My response was, "Yes, we have fought in previous lives," and I reminded her that I had always won our fights and will win this one in this life as well. I also stated, "I will overcome all that you will try to bring against me, and you will regret this!" As you can gather, this meeting did not end well. I knew that I had more power, more authority, and more strength in the spiritual than she did. The kicker for her was that she knew it too.

SOUTH SIDE

Fast-forward to after my deliverance. I was really struggling with reincarnation because I knew I had lived many lives in the past, and they were all so clear to me. Also, when reading the Bible, I realized that it said that there was no such thing as reincarnation. I took it before God and asked Him to clarify this for me. He said, "Shelve it, my child, until later." Six months later, my daughter came to me and said, "Mom, I still believe in reincarnation." I did not have any answers to her question because I too still believed in it. I took it before God again, and this time He showed me. He took me back to the time when the wife of the trucker and I were walking together on the land discussing our fights in previous lives. Then God powerfully showed me how the demons within us were talking through us both. It was the spirits in us that had fought each other in previous lives, not us humans. The scales dropped from my eyes, and my thoughts on this subject were now crystal clear—there is no reincarnation!

What had been within me had been so intertwined with me; why would I not get flashbacks of the lives I thought I had lived? It had been living in other people's bodies, besides mine, and obviously when the person dies or when Christ delivers them, it would go find another body to live in. Oh my God, look what you did for me. You took me out of hell.

Sometime later, when I went to Halifax to visit a family there, I spoke to a pastor. I felt led to tell him about God's explanation of reincarnation. The next morning, the pastor phoned me, thanking me because in secret he had believed in reincarnation, even though he was a pastor. After we spoke together and I shared more with him about my new realization on this topic, he did not believe in reincarnation anymore. God had set him free that night. He would now go on and set others free by the power of his testimony just as my testimony had set him free.

Dear Lord, thank you. Whoever reads this, remember there is absolutely no reincarnation; it is just demons living within you and you picking up the memory of the lives of the people that the demons had lived in.

CHAPTER 5

Don't Mess with Demons

Fred and I continued to run our businesses separately, even though our relationship was having a lot of problems. We were also socializing with the couple I had mentioned earlier, who had the same demonic background as I did. Of course, in all situations like this, there is an immediate connection between you and them. Life was interesting, to say the least. Many months into running the store, I was led by the spirits to buy ninety-seven acres of farmland not far from the store. I was led to buy this land in this particular area because it was spiritually holy. I found out afterwards that it was actually very unholy and spiritually unclean. The land was, sure enough, just like the spirits had told me, perfect. It was this perfect piece of land with its valleys, mounds, thorn trees, etc. The price was right, and we bought it.

I was doing what I was told to do. They were communicating with me every day. I was talking to them more than I was talking to my husband or my customers, and it was a daily dialogue as natural as talking to you. What I didn't have a clue about at the time was that this piece of land had a spiritual principality ruling over it, one who did not bow his knee to Christ. There was also a group of eight spiritual figures, which I will call the "circle of eight." They appeared to be men and wore monk's clothing. I never saw their faces. They started to appear in my life after buying the store. There was one that worked behind them all who was number nine and the leader.

Within a year of buying the land, I was led to build a dome-shaped house. The circle of eight had many discussions with me about exactly what they wanted, so we built a geometric dome or roundhouse. For what reason? I was told it was for the end-times. The end-times were explained to me by the group of eight as the end of time as described in Revelations. Who was I building the building for? My God? But which God was I serving? At the time, I didn't question any of this, I just did as I was told. As long as I did as I was told, there was always the money there to do what was needed. Everything was made easy for me, well, almost. My second husband came along for the ride.

Before the dome was constructed, the spirits informed me that my son would have to leave and go live with his father. I didn't agree with what they were telling me, but the pressure was put on me to let him go. I did not belong to myself, they really did own me. Their presence was felt in many ways. I was forced to pay attention to them. They tortured me from the inside by making me feel tremendous pain within my torso area. It felt like they were ripping my insides apart, but they were actually pulling my soul apart. They did this whenever I was not being obedient. In the end, I caved in and gave my son up to his father. I remember drinking alcohol for a week after trying to deaden my pain over my son.

I did not see my son again for about ten years after that. I made absolutely no contact with him at all. The spirits pulled whatever plugs they needed to make me do their will. As a person, I did not have normal human feelings, yet many other things would go my way. For example, if I wanted a parking space, one would become available to me, and I got what I asked for as long as it was in agreement to their plan. I was never really a child or a teenager. I was living my life according to their rules. At this stage in my life, I was being controlled by them completely; however, I would rebel from time to time, but they always got their way in the end.

As I look back on it now, I was experiencing nothing short of demon possession. In my life up to this point, I had tried to kill myself, I had three nervous breakdowns, I had nearly gone mad more than once, I was oppressed, and I was afflicted with phobias, panic attacks, and all sorts of other unpleasant things. All along, God and Jesus could have saved me, but the problem was that I didn't know this at the time. I lived my life onward upward and downward. I had to forget about my daughter and my son. I had work to do for my masters through the circle of eight. I really had no idea how deceived I was. I thought I was working for God, but unfortunately, I was wrong. It was satan, whom I was being led by, not God.

CHAPTER 6

How to Die but Still Be Alive

To kill the pain within me, I would beat my head against walls, pull my skin, and bite my tongue so it would hurt more than the hurt inside of me. Again, I felt I was spiraling out of control, just like years ago when I was struggling to look sane. During these turbulent times, I learned a valuable trick. I would drink alcohol because it deadened my emotions, and I could switch the spirits off in my brain. This allowed me to feel that I had some control over myself. There was a sort of relief there when I had alcohol in my body. I started to drink more as their pressure became more intense. I knew not to take drugs because I would have had absolutely no control at all over myself compared to using alcohol. I had such a sense that if I took drugs, I would not get back into my body. Regardless of how I tried to numb the pain, the spirits would punch me spiritually such that my spirit would be split into thousands of atoms. I would then try and grab them to collect them and bring them back into myself so I could look normal again. But I was losing bits of myself more and more as time went on. The spirits would constantly test me, and I would often rebel. I think I was a bit of an experiment to them. I am sure they have tortured many other people, just as I was.

The spirits would also give me a false sense of freedom and hope, and when like a dog I would beg for freedom, they would give me a treat for a second and then snatch it away from me. To me, I felt as if they were playing with me just like my father did. I was their pawn. They didn't like humans, anyway. Humans were just a means to an end. God uses his people to help his people. Demons use people to help them accomplish their evil deeds.

An interesting fact is that while the spirits were preparing for the end-times, using me to build the dome, they actually did not even know when the end-times would come. I did wonder about this at times, but now I know the difference between dark and light. The only one who knows when the end-times will come is God as in Revelations, which is a book in the Bible.

In my marriage to Fred, I was the spiritual leader in all aspects of our lives. Fred didn't like this. He was not as devoted to working on the dome as I was. Then one Friday, we had a huge confrontation. The spirit voices were very unhappy because he was not doing as he was told. He was angry, and they were angry; I was in the middle. They told me to confront him, and I did. Immediately, there was a high level of conflict. This was serious, and energies were flying high. They were more than upset with him, and through me they were coldly sarcastic to him. At one point, I thought my husband was going to hit me. He could sense their presence but couldn't see them, but he could see me. I was told to confront him again. I was getting fed up with being in the middle and the messenger, so I told them, "Do your own correcting and dirty work!" With that, I was instantly cast out of my body into a black hole. There were no stars, no light. You could liken it to the universe without the stars. I couldn't smell, see, or touch anything, yet I felt that I was attached to a cord coming from my navel.

My spirit was separated from my body, and I tried again and again to get back into my body. Each time, I was repelled back. I was in that hellish cold place for three days, entombed and so full of fear. When I was allowed back into my body, my husband was going to leave me, and my staff of four were going to quit. Whatever had overtaken my body carried on working in the store while I was gone; it was cold, cruel, and harsh.

On arriving back in my body, I was furious with my husband. I blamed him for what the spirits had just done to me. I told him if that ever happened to me again, I would do away with him. What happened to me was far worse than death. Did this bring us closer together? No! I felt my life was cursed but didn't understand why. Who was I, anyway? A nobody. What was normal in my life? Nothing.

I think I sorted the staff out and managed to carry on. The dome had to be ready for the end-times (whenever that was going to be). Did the spirits care what happened to us little humans? Of course not. I realized much later how much they hated us, but as long as we were useful, they put up with us. I had a job to complete under their supervision. At the time, I thought that I was born for such a time as this. Thank God my God loves me and saw me through all of this and much more by His awesome grace through Jesus Christ.

It was the spirits who taught me everything I knew at this point. They even taught me that Jesus was a prophet, a low prophet with no power. So here I was—I had money, power, and some influence. I was very spiritual (but on the wrong side), I had a husband, but I was far from happy. I had given my children up in obedience to them. I do not know how I survived, and the only thing I can think of now is that God had His hand on my life even then.

CHAPTER 7

Worthless Land and Whitewashed Walls

Aﬁer my deliverance several years later, my eyes were opened to God's truth. I was informed that the land that we were building our dome on was unholy and that certain ceremonies that God would have found detestable had been performed there. Things hung from the trees indicating that witchcraft was being used by men and women to conjure up evil powers.

Leviticus 19:31 says, "Do not turn to mediums or seek out spiritist's, for you will be defiled by them. I am the LORD your God."

"If a person turns to mediums and wizards, playing the harlot after them, I will set my face against that person, and will cut him off from among his people" (Leviticus 20:6).

"For example, never sacrifice your son or daughter as a burnt offering. And do not let your people practice fortune-telling or use sorcery, or interpret omens, or engage in witchcraft, or cast spells, or function as mediums or psychics, or call forth the spirits of the dead. Anyone who does these things is detestable to the LORD" (Deuteronomy 18:10–12).

Most of the above I was doing. Let me tell you satan is behind the occult. That is why God forbids His people to have anything to do with it.

"Finally, be strong in the Lord and in his mighty power. Put on the full armor of God so that you can take your stand against the devil's schemes. For our struggle is not against flesh and blood, but against the rulers, against the authorities, against the powers of this dark world and against the spiritual forces of evil in the heavenly realms. (Ephesians 6:10-12).

Yet another spiritual being was also communicating to me with an agenda for getting the dome ready for end-times. This particular spirit looked like a Quaker. He was dressed like one, even to having the tall black hat. I was getting such strong visions of the end-times.

I also had a spiritual bodyguard whenever I was at the dome. He looked like the big hairy creature in *Star Wars*. He was at least nine feet tall. He never spoke but guarded me. I saw him at the dome at first, and then later he even joined me at the store. I just knew he was a silent presence there to protect me. He was part of my spooky life and probably never would have been allowed to stay if my other spirit group hadn't wanted him there.

Near the dome, there was a tourist attraction called Southwold Prehistoric Earthworks. The spirits would send me there to pray against their enemies (which now I know were Christians). I only knew I was praying against enemies. One night, while I was down there praying, I saw a vision. I instinctively knew that it was Jacob's ladder. The ladder came down from the heavens, and angels descended the ladder to let me know that this was a blessed place. (See picture opposite)

I realize now that it was an unholy place blessed by evil. They used the same images from the Bible, to keep me convinced that it was all real and pure and not evil. They always led me to believe that I was working for God. Across from the Earthworks, there was a Christian camp. I can say with all honesty that I never ever saw the camp with the word *Christian* on the sign until God had delivered me. When I did see it years later, I thought they had just built it. I had been down there dozens of times and never saw it. The scales had dropped from my eyes.

The building of the dome was approximately one and a half miles into the land in a hollow surrounded by trees. So far, things were going according to the spirits' plans.

The dome had three levels—the underground, the main floor, and then half a floor on top. The main window was a five-pointed star with two points pointing upwards. This means that it was the sign of the goat or satan, so this window was a satanic star. There were two triangular windows at the top of the dome, and each side of the star window were three other square windows. The glass for the windows were all special order and expensive. When the special windows arrived, the company wouldn't deliver them to the dome because the road was rough. My second husband and I loaded the glass into our van and strapped them firmly in place, and then as we went to drive off the lot at the store, all the straps broke, and the windows were smashed. I thought this was the enemy at work. It was the devil working to stop me from building the dome. In actual fact, it was God who was trying to stop me from installing the glass for the totally evil window. So, I reordered the panes of glass again. When the spirits started discussing the shape of the window to me, I said I didn't like it because it looked evil. It was a discussion that went on for three days, and in the end, they convinced me that the window was good and not evil. *That I since discovered was a lie from hell.*

The outside of the dome had gray tiles on the roof and white-washed walls. I tried to grow poppies there, and no matter what seeds I used or earth I put down to grow them, not one poppy ever grew there. The only thing that seemed to grow well on the land were thorn trees, bramble bushes, and thistles.

There were many strange things that happened down at the dome, but one incident my children and I remember very well. Fred and I decided to have our annual staff party down at the dome. We organized tables and chairs, food, a barbecue, drinks, and games for people to play, and some people planned to stay overnight in the dome. I invited all of my staff and their husbands and some close friends. My daughter and son were also there. My son mixed the drinks, and it was a beautiful sunny summer day. That is about all we remember. Nobody can remember what happened that day. Granted many of us were drinking alcohol, but what was strange was that the next day and the days that followed this party, no one seemed to remember anything of what happened. It was like a void. Yet time did pass. We started the party at around noon, and we all stayed there until late into the night. A good ten hours of partying and no one remembers anything?

My daughter had prepared items for various games to be played such as the three-legged race, an egg and spoon race, sack race, and prizes, but the next day, all of these items were just sitting where they were left. Nobody played any games. My daughter still to this day can't believe that no one remembers anything from that party. She worked for me at the time and knew the staff well. She asked many people who were there that day what had happened, trying to fill in the gaps, and every person admitted that they didn't remember anything. *Weird?*

Hebrews 6: 7-8 (NIV) says, "Land that drinks in the rain often falling on it and that produces a crop useful to those from whom it is farmed received the blessing of God. But land that produces thorns and thistles is worthless and is in danger of being cursed. In the end it will be burned."

After my deliverance, God gave me this scripture concerning the dome. "This will happen because these evil prophets (demons) deceived my people by saying," 'All is peaceful' when there is no peace at all! It's as if the people have built a flimsy wall, and these prophets are trying to reinforce it by covering it with whitewash! Tell these whitewashers that their wall will soon fall down. A heavy rainstorm will undermine it; great hailstones, and mighty winds will knock it down. And when the wall falls, the people will cry out, 'What happened to your whitewash?' Therefore, this is what the Sovereign Lord says: "I will sweep away your whitewashed wall with a storm of indignation, with a great flood of anger, and with hail stones of fury. I will break down your wall right to its foundation, and when it falls, it will crush you. Then you will know that I am the Lord. At last my anger against the wall and those who covered it with whitewash will be satisfied. Then I will say to you: 'The wall and those who whitewashed it are both gone. They were lying prophets (demons) who claimed peace would come to Jerusalem when there was no peace. I, the Sovereign LORD, have spoken!' (Ezekiel 13:10–16, Life Applications Study Bible).

My Father God showed me that the prophets referred to in this quote were the demons and evil spirits. God did not destroy the spirits until he had taken me out and away from that evil place. This scripture I was given by the Lord sums up well how the land was being prepared for evil purposes.

CHAPTER 8

Reversing a Curse and Amazing Grace

The spirits told me I would die at the age of sixty and that I would go to an amazing place in the afterworld, which was being prepared for me. People and animals would serve me. I would have my own temple, and in it would be the best of everything. Doesn't sound like hell, does it? But that is where I would have been going, one-way ticket and no stopping for second chances. My training in all things spiritual continued, and now much of my memory of this era of my life has been taken away from me by the Lord.

God must have been working behind the scenes in my life, even though I didn't see or feel Him. There was an incident I need to tell you about. There was a young man in the village where I had the store, as far as I (and a lot of other people) thought he was a man of troubled character. He did drugs, was abusive, got young girls pregnant, had a history of stealing—name it and he did it with no regrets. Two girls who were sisters both thought they were in love with him. He played one against the other. It seemed that they were always in the store when things concerning them and him were playing out. It would have been much better had I not seen this going on. I thought it would be a lot better if he was just not around anymore, so I cursed him. I thought he was garbage and then blanked my mind and forgot completely about the incident.

A couple of days later, a man whom I knew came into the store, all white in the face and shaking. He said, "I have to speak with you, Gloria." I took him into the office where we could talk privately. He said to me, "I had a vision, and there were three tombstones, and on one of them was the name of the young man I had cursed." I thought he was lying. He then said, "You have done something against him, and you need to correct it." I just laughed and shrugged it off. He then became more persistent and would not let it go. He said, "Unless you undo what you have done, this is going to be bad for you." I said to him, "Do I look scared?" I then asked him to leave the store.

Here was a man who was into witchcraft and sorcery along with his wife who both claimed they had a connection with the spirit world. He was very scared, frightened, and nervous with what he had seen in his vision about me. Did my spirits tell me to correct what I had done? No! Did I even feel anything? No! Consciously, had I done something evil? No! It was done as it was thought, so shall it be and now it is finished. What happened over the next twenty-four hours had to have been from God and God alone.

I went to bed that night, but I was very restless. At two in the morning, the phone rang and woke me up. Normally, I would never answer the phone that late at night. Guess who it was? It was one of the sisters. She was terribly upset that this young man preferred her sister over her and asked me if I would come over and talk with her. So, at two thirty in the morning, I went over to her house. At the time, I had something come over me that felt very different emotionally from when my spirits were around. I realize now it must have been the Lord.

The girl wanted to take her life, she was pregnant, and there was such a powerful presence in the room, which was different from what I had experienced before. The energy was warm and loving compared to the usual cold and harsh energy I always felt. There was also a sweetness in the room, and you could almost smell something that smelled like apple blossoms, which amazed me at the time because her home was far from clean. For a period of time, I was changed, and so was she. As the hours rolled by, we talked about this man who was causing her so much grief and on whom I had put a curse. She was venting to me about him. As she was talking about him, my feelings towards him changed drastically. I started to feel like he was my best friend and that I would have died for him. I saw why he did the things he did, his history was not good, and I learnt to love that young man. Whatever I had cursed him with was taken away when I felt love for him. I had to speak it out loud. I even asked for forgiveness for cursing him. I had to lift the curse, and so the curse was removed.

I ended up leaving the house at six thirty in the morning and headed back to the store. Neither the girl nor myself ever talked about the incident again. Only after my deliverance did I realize for sure that it was Jesus who was in the room with us that night. I did not need the consequences of what I had done to that young man on my soul. So much love surrounded me that night that I had undone the evil with Jesus guiding me. Just remember, all this happened, and I wasn't even saved yet. I still do not know completely the impact of all the events that happened that night. It was very powerful and certainly of God. Great was the evil, but greater was the Lord's love for the girl, the guy I cursed, and myself. It was a miracle. I had never felt so much love for someone who was, in my opinion, a loser. This incident made me aware for the first time in my life of a different kind of power. It was so unlike anything I had experienced before with my spirit friends.

CHAPTER 9

I Am Invincible

The spare room in my apartment above the store was my sanctuary. It was approved of by the spirits. Here I would pray against God's enemies. Now remember the god I served was satan. I was totally deceived. God showed me after my crossing over from dark to light that I was praying against His people. This I did not realize. I was told to pray against God's enemies, and faithfully I did. I prayed before the full moon and just after the full moon. I burnt incense, and this was completed every month at certain times and on special days, just like in the Bible. See Isaiah 1:14–15, as you read this, these were God's people and look what God was saying: "I hate your new moon celebrations and your annual feasts. They are a burden to me, I cannot stand them! When you lift up your hands in prayer I will not look. Though you offer many prayers I will not listen, for your hands are covered with the blood of innocent victims."

I thought I was doing God's will for His glory. I was actually doing it for the enemy of our souls (satan). I even fasted. When I fasted, my spirits told me to eat fruit or drink fruit juices but no meat. I had no difficulty fasting. My spirits told me it was for purity of the body, spirit, and mind. The spirits taught me about other religious teachers, such as Gautama who was given the name of Buddha.

I also met other ancient religious teachers in the spiritual, some who were Indian gods and goddesses. Jesus, God's son, was way down at the bottom of the list of religious teachers. The following is taken from *The Facts on the Occult* by T. Ankerberg and J. Weldon (P.26).

Philosopher, trail attorney, and noted theologian Dr. John Warwick Montgomery has authored or edited several books on the occult. He warns that there is a definite correlation between negative occult activity and madness. European psychiatrist L. Szondi has shown a high correlation between involvement in spiritualism and occultism (and the related theosophical blind alleys) on the one hand and schizophrenia on the other. The tragedy of most sorcery, invocation of demons, and related practices is that those who carry on these activities refuse to face the fact that they always turn out for the worst. What is received through the Faustian past never satisfies, and one pays with one's soul in the end, anyway.

My point on this is that you may look like a winner in the occult, but in reality you are always a loser. The only way back to "normal" is to let God, Jesus Christ, and the Holy Spirit into your life before it is too late. "Do not be deceived."

Beware of who you pray to. Who enlightens you? Who do you pray to? What is feeding you spiritually? There is only one God, one Jesus, and one Holy Spirit. Before God delivered me, I was a puppet with almost no will of my own. I was being taught to be obedient to the spirit world. I was taught to masquerade a part, *but I am no longer theirs*, for now I am free and have tasted Christ and all that the trinity stands for. The trinity is God, Christ Jesus, and the Holy Spirit. The spirits were hard taskmasters; they were slave drivers. What an inheritance! It was a den of inequity. There was no chance of being rescued (but God had a plan for me).

I used to make trips to Toronto and buy semiprecious stones and crystals. What was in me showed me the ones to pick. Also, they had me pick certain artifacts. To buy them money was no object, so in my sanctuary, very special items were picked to place on a chest I had in the room. There was a picture on the wall above the chest. It was a picture of a female black wolf with piercing and evil eyes. The wolf is walking towards the observer, right out of the picture.

I bought the artifacts from people in Toronto who thought I was a professor at one of the universities because I was very knowledgeable about the pieces I bought. It was what was inside of me that knew what to buy. It was extremely intelligent and intellectual. Why would it not have been? It was probably hundreds of years old. In fact, after God delivered me, it was quite a shock to my system to find out that I was not as intelligent and intellectual as I thought I was. When I was delivered of the spirits, all of that knowledge went with them. God always knows what is good for you and what it is that you really need. The spirits pressed all my buttons, which is totally different when you belong to God. He gives you free will. You make choices. Don't be deceived. Don't deceive yourself where sin is concerned.

So many times I saw a chessboard. God on one side, satan on the other. All of us people are the pawns. Let us play the game our God wants for us, less of us, more of Him so that in Him we win. satan has power, but we do not have to be his victims through bad choices. Ask the Holy Spirit to help you the right way. If the Holy Spirit did it for me, He would most certainly do it for you. He loves us so much, so much more than we can fully fathom. You open yourself up to sin when you choose to abuse things such as alcohol, prescription or street drugs, having sex with anybody, and other things deadlier.

I was conditioned to think that I was invincible and could not be defeated in this world or the next. Whatever wall came up in front of me, I could walk through it and win glory for the wrong god. I would buy and bless semiprecious stones such as topaz, carbuncle, turquoise, agate, amethyst, beryl, onyx, and jasper. There were other stones, but they were more expensive, such as rubies and emeralds. Crystals came alive in my hands and would sparkle and glow.

What was in me thought very highly of itself and made me feel like I was a priestess of highborn nobility in the spiritual. It didn't look so highly on witches and wizards, yet they were important to their master's cause. The master here is satan. The demons fought amongst each other within the different levels. But when called to attention against God's people, each one knew its place and would come as one against them to overcome and displace Christians. They give no quarter in a battle and take no prisoners.

Whenever I was sent into battle either spiritually or in the flesh, I always won my battles. Later God told me, "Yes, you did always win your battles but you were being conditioned, and what would have happened to you if you had been put into battle against a true Holy Spirit-filled Christian or against my angels?" I don't think I would have won my battle but would have probably died and gone straight to hell, not heaven.

I would carry a certain amount of semiprecious stones with me as I travelled with my husband, giving them out as instructed by the spirit that was inside of me. People would even stop me in the streets, saying I just know you have a word for me. Most of the time, I would have a word for them, and I would give them a stone or a crystal blessing it. What I was doing I likened to a guru (or teacher). The spirit within me was teaching and leading these people. It knew it could trap them into its web using me as a decoy. So many strange things happened. Again, after my deliverance, I didn't want to touch semiprecious stones ever again.

God spoke to me about this after my crossover. "My child, I first created everything. Unfortunately, the enemy has used the stones for evil. Don't be afraid." Then He showed me a high priest's breastplate, which contained twelve semiprecious stones upon it—all of the same types of stones I had used on the dark side. God showed me how the high priest was called upon to discern God's will by the use of the Urim and Thurim and how the jewels symbolically represented the whole Israelite nation (twelve stones and twelve tribes of Israel). Also, the semiprecious stones were set in gold in the priest's breastplate. I would never have known this if God had not shown me. After this, I no longer was afraid of gold, silver, semiprecious stones, and crystals of any kind. My God had created the semiprecious stones first. Seeing this truth, I was totally set free.

CHAPTER 10

A Prisoner in My Own Body

After becoming a Christian, I was terribly concerned about what had happened to all those talismans, stones, and crystals I had given out to people under the power of the wrong god. They could be potentially dangerous to people and should not be in anyone's possession. I felt that people who possessed such items risk having their life jinxed. I also believed that negative forces could more easily influence their lives, and this negativity and evil could spread unless the items were destroyed.

God then showed me what He had done to counteract this. One of my customers had bought quite a large selection of crystals from me and was very interested in all that I did. One day, she telephoned me and wanted to talk about the crystals because she thought they had died. I had her bring them into the store, and I looked at them. She asked me, "What did I see?" What I saw was amazing. All of the crystals had lost their light and glow. God had snuffed out the evil light within the crystals. Wow! Here was God showing me His power. I asked her if she wanted her money back, and she replied, "No, I just wanted you to know that I don't believe in this worthless stuff anymore." Then she left.

Here God was showing me how *all* of the crystals and talismans I had given out over the years had come to naught under His hand. Everything was now powerless. *All power* had gone from all of the pieces I had ever sold or given out. I knew people would not remember what had been said to them, all had been covered in the blood of Jesus. My guilt was gone. What had been in me was using its guile to deceive people, and it had now been washed away. My Father had snuffed the evil light out from the crystals. I was so thankful to God; He washed away all of the dark power within those crystals and talismans, cleansing all those people I had touched.

An interesting incident happened one time when Fred and I went to the States looking for equipment for a new tattoo business he wanted to start. We arrived late at night to meet the owner of the business, and I was left by myself in the living room. It was really dark in the room. Before the guy went off to talk to my husband, he told me he had two cats and that the female was fine but in no way was I to touch the bigger male cat. He told me he was vicious and hated strangers. I thought okay, fine. I asked for a light to be put on in the living room, so a side table light was put on. Suddenly, I had a strange feeling that somebody was watching me. I looked around, and there in the shadows, I saw two eyes watching me. As I made eye contact with it, it came out of the shadows towards me. It was a huge black cat, the one I was warned about. It was the vicious one! As he came towards me, he was purring. In my language, that means friendly cat. So, I held out my hands to him, and he sat at my feet looking up at me. I patted him on the head, and he jumped into my lap. He was really heavy. He then curled up on my lap, looking at me with adoration.

Meanwhile, the guy came back into the room and jumped back, horrified that the cat was in my lap. He couldn't believe it. He said that he had never seen his cat sit on a stranger's lap before. I realize now that what was in me easily had power over that cat, and the cat saw it. It didn't worship me, just the thing that was in me.

Earlier in the year, while it was still winter, I needed a holiday. I was depressed, and my life was in turmoil. My husband, daughter, and I went to Niagara Falls for three days and two nights. Darice drove her own car, and we drove ours. It was great, but coming home, Fred and I were involved in a terrible car accident, which was not our fault. It was winter, but coming home, the roads were good with one lane of traffic either side. I had taken my seat belt off to go into a store and had not put it back on. A car coming the opposite way saw a gas station, didn't see our car, turned in front of us, and crashed right into us. The driver of the other car was fine, and his passenger had a broken arm. My husband was fine, but I was not so good. Not being belted in the car, my face hit the dashboard, and all of the bones were broken across my face.

I was taken to Grimsby Hospital where they tried to take X-rays. I had a concussion, and they had a hard time getting X-rays because of the state I was in. My face would stay swollen for nearly a year after this accident, and the doctor saw me the next day and told me I just had a broken nose and that I would be fine. I was released from hospital with my face five times its normal size. My husband couldn't even look at me. Also, I could not hear my voices, nothing was coming through. It was arranged for us to be driven back to the store and our home. I started getting strange nosebleeds. My eye was being pulled down, and my face looked grotesque. My husband didn't want anything to do with me. I was struggling, and where were my voices that were always there for me I was alone and rejected and again in a very dark place.

I came home on a Tuesday and saw the family doctor on the Wednesday. My doctor told me I was being vain and worried about the bump on my nose. I lost it with him (no one knew that my jaw was also broken). I screamed at him as best as I could and told him that I would never be back to his office. I couldn't eat or lie back on a pillow without feeling really dizzy. When I laid back, it felt as if everything in my face was loose and floating, and the nosebleeds continued. That night, I had such a bad nosebleed I had soaked my pillow in blood. The pains in my face and head were very severe.

I felt so alone. The next day, I was still in so much pain when I went to see the surgeon at the local hospital. After examining me, he said, "Do you realize how badly hurt you are?" At this point, I couldn't even cry properly, thank goodness someone realized how badly injured I was. On Friday, I was admitted to a downtown hospital for surgery to my battered face. The two surgeons had asked me to bring photos of myself, full face and sideways, so they had an idea of what I had looked like. To me, things were not going well. I made sure my husband came to the hospital with me, but then he left without even saying good-bye. The loneliness I felt was terrifying. Who was there for me? One of the doctors was a cosmetic surgeon. They took numerous X-rays and said they were going to have to re-break certain bones that were already healing in my face. When they operated, they would probably cut under my chin and my eyes to reconstruct my face. Voices, where are you? Husband, where are you? Where was I? In pain and in a black void.

After a bad day of being examined, I was resting in my room, and a nurse's aide came in. While I didn't have my voices this nurse's aide came in and started talking to me, telling me things she couldn't have possibly known about me. Through her my spirits comforted me; they told me I was not going to die and that they had too much for me to do yet. I would overcome all that was in front of me. They also said not to worry about my husband or other people because they themselves would look out for me. My spirits obviously couldn't reach me through the usual inner channels. The following night, I was awake and could not sleep. The spirit of my grandmother came into my room and spoke to me and stayed with me most of the night. It really wasn't my grandmother, I realize now, but an entity using the form of my dead grandmother whom I had loved dearly.

The following morning, I was set to be operated on at eight in the morning, but it didn't happen. The hospital had an emergency. Four men were badly hurt in a car accident. I was left on hold. The doctor said we were still set for my operation that day, but I didn't know when. That was a very long day. I phoned my husband, but he wouldn't come to the phone, saying he was busy. I was not allowed any food, and I was very scared. It was now eight in the evening and still no word about the operation. I phoned my husband again; he was upset that I had called him, and he put the phone down on me. I gave myself a long talking to. "Okay, Gloria, you have been here before. So what? Tomorrow is another day. Things will be better tomorrow." It was now ten forty-five, same night. Then I got word. "Okay, time for surgery." I said to the doctors, "Hold it! You must be tired. It is very late. I don't think it is a good idea." But they said that the surgery *had* to be done now. They had to operate fast because my bones were already setting into place.

The next morning, I woke up in the recovery room. I was told that they could not finish the operation because I had stopped breathing. So, they still had to wire my jaw shut so it could heal properly. There were no cuts on my face, and that was a miracle. The surgeons had worked up through my mouth and up my nose. Wires were coming out of each side of my face just below where my temple was. Everything was broken across my face and had to be wired in place. There were buttons attached to the wires so that each day the wires could be adjusted. Boy, did I look lovely. Yet the best was yet to come.

Later that day, with one nurse holding me down and a doctor and another nurse working on my very tender mouth, they wired my jaws together. They couldn't give me any pain medication because my body had already had too much. So, I endured all this without being sedated. I never want to go through that ordeal again! The surgeons were very pleased with the outcome of the operation. They told me later that I was in their Book of Record with photos, etc. This operation was unlike any that they had ever performed before. That statement did not impress me. What was I going to do? What was I going to look like? It took approximately three months before I started to hear my voices again. But during this time, it gave me time to think about the tremendous amount of things that had gone sadly wrong in my life thus far. What was happening inside of me? I had no contentment, no joy, no light. By not having the voices, I was left to my own devices, and I was able to see and come to terms with some of the abuse I had taken from them, trying hard to understand things!

Many times I was in dire distress, and nobody could help me. I was a prisoner in my own body. I was just an empty shell. One day shortly after I got out of the hospital, I watched a geographic nature program showing a wasp laying her eggs inside a living caterpillar.

The eggs would hatch and eat the caterpillar from the inside out while the caterpillar was still alive. I vomited. It reminded me of my own situation. It made me sick.

My husband was jealous of the attention people were giving me. I wanted out of the hospital, I felt so trapped. I wasn't sure of anything. I was in the hospital just over a week, and I told them they would have to sedate me if they wanted me to stay. I was told that I had to be sure that I didn't faint and fall forward and hurt my face in any way. I was also to stay on liquids for food for six weeks. They gave me special pliers in case I choked because remember my jaw was wired shut. I was given a plastic mask for the half of my face to protect it from harm. The doctors worried that I might feel weak being on a liquid diet, and I could fall easily. They really did not want me to go home so soon, but I insisted. It was important for me to remain sane.

As soon as I got back in my apartment at the store, I decided to go back to work despite looking scary. My right-hand girl asked me to not work in the store because I was scaring people, especially children, but I insisted on working. It actually was good for business because word got out about how freaky I looked, and although people were kind and considerate to me during this time, everyone had to have a look. My daughter said that I was the spitting image of Frankenstein's wife. Regardless, I really needed to get "back up" and work. It brought me back to some kind of sanity. I also had to work hard to get my memory back. My face remained swollen for over nine months. I was a mess inside and out. I had to go back to work to keep myself together.

Meanwhile, I was getting deeper and deeper into darkness. Life with my second husband was going downhill fast. Fred had lost all interest in me at this point. The girls who worked for me told me later that during the time I was in the hospital, he had been hitting on them and flirting, and they were certain that he had a girlfriend. I suspected he was seeing someone else as well because he was normally somewhat of a shabby dresser, and now suddenly he had new clothes and was wearing aftershave regularly—things he had never done before. When I got home, he told me that he wanted to get into the tattoo supply business in a big way. He even got a tattoo put on his arm. I never liked tattoos. Oddly enough, what was inside of me didn't like tattoos either. To buy into the tattoo business, we used money from the store. The store was making a good living, and we were being blessed by what was spiritually unholy, I might add, so we used the money for the dome and other projects.

At the local bank, we had a separate account with $36,000 in it. It was in both of our names. When we had agreed to start the tattoo business, the agreement was to not touch the $36,000 we had in a special account. The spirits were quite happy to have my second husband run this business, as it kept him out of their hair but not out of mine. The tattoo business was beginning to do well, and then my husband wanted to organize a catalog, which would display all the products he would be selling in his business. My husband had big ideas; he wanted the catalog to be in color and have expensive paper. This was going to cost a considerable amount of money. He didn't seem to mind the expense, but I did. He wanted to use the $36,000 we had in the bank, even though this was not what we had agreed to. I knew we were heading for a separation and divorce, so I wanted to be sure I would have my half of that $36,000.

One day, we had to drive to the lawyer's office together because suddenly there was an interest in me again since I could be worth up to $350,000 in damages. Money talks. I challenged him on this point as we were driving away from the lawyer's office. Now remember my mouth was still wired. He came back at me very cold and cuttingly. I figured, let us have another accident! In frustration, I took off my long leather glove and swiped him hard across his face while he was driving. We nearly went off the road.

I slowly recovered physically from the accident, but I was not too sure about my mental state. I worked hard to keep my sanity. My husband surprised me by never attempting to leave, even though our relationship was very shaky at the time, and I knew that he had a girlfriend on the side. Due to a potential settlement through the courts, Fred stayed in the relationship. If they declared that I had brain damage, Fred would be in charge of the money and taking care of me. No way was I going to let that happen.

Four years after the car accident, the lawyers and the doctors in charge of my case set up appointments for me to go and see a specialist to determine if I had brain damage. I was to be tested over three days. Fred was happy and thrilled. The thought of us (me) receiving so much money potentially and then having to look after my well-being made him very happy. For four years, I stayed in that relationship while I healed, knowing he was sleeping around, but I chose to ignore it because I had bigger issues to deal with. First day of testing, I did everything I was told. For example, there were games to see how my brain was working. Second day of testing, the specialist told me that I would find it difficult to execute my duties with regards to running the store and the staff as I had been. He said many other things afterwards as well, but to this day, I do not remember what he said. I did indeed feel brain-dead from time to time. When the specialist told me I was going to have major difficulties functioning in my business, I left his office abruptly. I couldn't handle what he was telling me. He reminded me as I walked out the door to come back the next day for more testing.

I walked from his office downtown, dazed and confused. I thought about dying and thought that would be easier than dealing with all of this. I was crying the entire time. What was worse was that I couldn't even trust my husband anymore. I certainly didn't expect him to come and pick me up after my appointment, but suddenly on that day, he was free, and he willingly came and picked me up, as I was not allowed to drive. Previously, he would avoid me at all costs. Back at the store, my manager asked me what was wrong with me because my eyes were swollen from crying, and I was very upset.

She came up to the apartment with me, and I told her what the specialist had said to me. She said to me very directly, "Gloria, you have always been like this, a little strange and weird. This is the way we have always known you. Don't let Fred and the lawyer try to make you think you are brain-dead and get money for it!" Then she left. What a night I had. I was up all night fighting many conflicting ideas and emotions about what was happening and where it was all taking me. I was trying to keep a balance in myself. Everyone around me was telling me I was damaged goods, and if I believed the lie, I was going to be in big trouble and not in control of my life. I was fighting for myself! I spoke firmly to myself, "I will succeed in these conflicts and will come out ahead and not be buried alive. Keep it simple, Gloria." So, I did come to a simple decision, and this was what I decided.

The next morning, I phoned the specialist and told him it was my husband and my lawyer who had the brain damage. He was no help to me as he was agreeing with Fred and the lawyer, and so I was not going to be there for any more evaluations. But I would make appointments for my husband and my lawyer. I then phoned my lawyer and told him the same thing and no more talking of getting $350,000-plus for my injuries. I spoke to my husband and told him what I thought of him and that I felt he needed to see the specialist. That put the cat amongst the pigeons, but it put me back on my feet and in the driver's seat of my life. Fred and I had a huge fight, but I felt stronger and more empowered. The lawyers washed their hands off me. I really didn't care.

I had no idea how I looked to my staff and customers. Once again, I was fighting for my life and my soul. I was trying as best as I could to keep myself altogether. It was hell, but I came through it. I refused to let anyone tell me that I was disabled in any way. Why would I let my husband, who didn't love me anymore, have a trust fund for $350,000 to look after me? Remember the $36,000 that my husband and I had in a joint account? It was money from the store that we had both made. We were in Toronto buying for the store when he told me that he was going to use some of the money to pay for the catalogue and spend the rest as he wanted to! Upon hearing this, I was furious. He just told me that he didn't care what I thought, he was going to spend the money on the catalog whether I like it or not. I thought, *Well, I am not going to tell you what I am going to do with that money.*

The next day, I withdrew the money from our account using a bank draft put in my name. I took it back to the store and placed it under the carpet in our bedroom so he would walk on it every single day and night and wouldn't know where it was. Revenge? Yes, perhaps. But no. Actually, I wanted to make sure I received my half of that $36,000 before he just spent it all leaving me with nothing. This action gave me a big boost. The same week I had a 2nd appointment with a leading psychiatrist at the Mental Institute in London.

This was part of a general check up on everything regarding the car accident. I remember I had to go through a mountain of checkups concerning my eyes, ears, nose and brain.

I told this psychiatrist what I had done with the money but not where I had hidden it because I wanted him to know that I was still mentally sane and capable of making plans. His eyes just got bigger and bigger. He wanted to know why I was telling him all this. My reply was, "I am telling you this because I might get hurt by my husband." The psychiatrist wanted to know where the money was hidden, but I would not tell him this. I wanted him to be a witness in case something happened. At the end of my appointment, he laughed and said, "You are not my usual patient and good luck to you and be careful!"

A few weeks later, Fred went to the bank to get the money out to pay for his catalog. The bill was $13,000. There was a huge uproar when he returned to the store. Why? Well, I had the money. After the store closed, we had a big fight. He lunged at me a few times. He so badly wanted to hurt me. I said to him, "If you touch me, you will never know where the money is." He ended up borrowing the money from his mother to get his tattoo catalogs produced. It didn't matter to me, our relationship was done, done, done. We were under the same roof still, but it was murder trying to live together.

I received my money from the accident. It was $53,000 plus expenses. This was put in my account, and I made sure that even if Fred and I separated, he could not touch it. The same was made clear to him by the lawyers. My daughter was staying with us for a while; it was around Christmas time and very cold. Fred was moving his stuff out, and I knew he would be going to his girlfriend's place. It was very foggy that evening. As he was about to leave, he turned to me and said, "Would you like me to stay?" I yelled at him, "So you can screw me and your girlfriend? I don't think so!" With that, he left. My daughter said to me, "Wow, Mom, it is all over!" And I said, "No, not tonight. He will be back." She said, "How do you know?" I was laughing and said, "Because it is so foggy out he won't be able to find his way over to his girlfriend's place." Sure enough, about an hour later, he came back and said he was going to sleep on the sofa. He then left the next day, telling everyone that I had thrown him out.

CHAPTER 11

Who Gave Them Permission?

I was beginning to wonder if my voices were good or evil. Having become doubtful of my voices during the last few years, I got thinking about who they were and on which side they were on. The fog within me was still not completely clear, though. I had always felt like my insides were being consumed, and I had an upset stomach all of the time. I felt like I had ulcers. I started to drink more alcohol to cut out the sound of my voices and to deal with life.

The spirits were also using my body for sexual purposes. They had been doing this for some time now, but I buried this realization deep within me. For example, I would be asleep in bed, and then I would be woken by the realization that something had gotten into bed with me, or sometimes I would wake up, and it was already having sex with me. It was creepy! Spirits having sex with people is not as isolated as one might think when you walk on the dark side or dabble in things you don't understand. You are vulnerable to spirits who can and will infiltrate your body. You may not be able to see them, but you can feel and smell them. You can also feel their hands all over your body. Don't dabble with this stuff. Don't bite the bait, they have set to trap you. You will receive more than you bargained for.

The store continued to be busy after Fred had left. I had half of the store painted black after he finally left, and I thought it looked fabulous. My spirits were drawing me in more and more. Often when I would speak to people, it was the spirits speaking through me. I was breaking down under all the pressures I had in my life. I enjoyed my job because it kept me sane. Here was something I knew I could do, and I did it well—running a business. I went to trade shows in Toronto to buy products for the store. I had several good staff, and I lost myself in my work. The atmosphere in the store was heavy because of what was in me. I was like a wind-up puppet—they could wind me up or wind me down. The store continued to be a hub of activity and prospered. The *owner* had the problems.

Looking back on my life, there were times when I didn't care if I lived or died. I put myself in harm's way. Vividly, I remembered this incident. It was a winter's day, and I am driving to the city. The portion of the road I was driving on is straight for four miles. Ahead of me, I see a line of traffic coming towards me. There were about seven cars. They were coming fast. My side of the road was clear. I too was moving fast. Then one car starts overtaking all the other cars. I was thinking, *You should not be doing that. Don't you see me on this side of the road?* So instead of slowing down, I accelerated. Everything is coming up fast. I wanted to hit the car.

To this day, I don't know how his car got back into line before we would have hit each other head on. I felt quite high from doing it. I was fed up with living, and I thought, *Well, let's put my life to the test. Am I going to live or to die?* Alas, I lived another day. My thought was about the other guy, that it would have served him right if there had been an accident. Go figure. That was my thinking at that time! I wondered if that had scared him. I bet it did.

CHAPTER 12

Searching for a Dream

I was running the store on my own, and at the same time, I continued to be demonized by spirits. The forces within me had almost completely nullified my capacity to think my own thoughts. However, there was still enough of my spirit left in me that I would often be in a power play between them and me. My life was becoming more and more theirs. What words do you use to explain this? Whom do you speak to about this? How can you be cured and stay cured? I really didn't know what I was into. There was a high-level principality and territorial spirits that I was also very aware of. I likened myself to Waterloo Station at rush hour. How many spirits did I "house"? How many used me or worked through me? With battle after battle, my spirits and demons tested me. They would then leave me alone until my strength was built up again. How far could they go to test my strength? I still lived above the store. After hours, that place was as busy as it was by day. Things moved, noises came out of nowhere. Chairs were pulled across the floor. I saw it so often I was desensitized by it all.

The spiritual activity in me was driving me crazy. I went to see a doctor at the local clinic. I told him I was not on any medication or using street drugs of any kind. I said I needed to use him as a sounding board so I wouldn't go mad. He taped the interview without my approval. I told him about my life. I was there maybe one to two hours. He asked me if I needed a prescription for my nerves, and I said, "No thanks and good-bye." The tape was evidently played back to the senior doctor of the clinic who phoned me and told me to come and see them again. The senior doctor looked at me as if I had ten heads. He asked me to give him a list of drugs I must have been taking, and with my permission, he would like to do a study of them and me. I left and never looked back. What was the point? I lived with things that people could not see or understand. After speaking to the doctor, I felt better telling someone. I went back to trying to stay composed, controlling my feelings, and trying not to get the demons upset.

While I was living on my own and running the business, I still had to deal with the fallout from Fred, who, of course, had left a few months ago. We were hashing out terms of the divorce proceedings, and he was well established with his new girlfriend. We had a dispute over our vehicles. We had three vehicles, and when he left, he took two of them; the third vehicle was a blue truck. I said to him, "I am keeping this one because it was easier for me to drive, and I would need to get supplies for the store." He was not happy about me having this truck. I felt the truck belonged to me, and it was the only vehicle I had. There had been times when I was in this vehicle, and I would go into a semi trance-like state, and it would drive itself. There was a lot of spiritual mayhem in and around this blue truck.

Due to Fred's persistence in wanting this truck, I decided to have the locks changed on the doors *and* the ignition. One night, Fred came over with his girlfriend and was saying that he was now going to take the truck. I didn't say anything. He went out to the parking lot and tried to unlock the door. He couldn't get in, so he smashed the window, got into the truck, and then tried to start the engine. Still it didn't work. He came flying back into the store in a rage, so much so that the police were called. The police filed it as a domestic dispute, and he left without my truck.

The next incident with this truck involved him asking to borrow the truck, saying he had some stuff to move from his house. It was a terrible winter's day with ice on the roads. I told him he was not having the truck unless I drove it, so we actually left in the truck together. He was not happy with me. We drove out to his mother's house, picked a table up, and delivered it to his girlfriend's place. Meanwhile, my manager was very concerned for me. She called the police, informing them of what was going on just in case something happened to me. So, after moving the table for him, we came back to the store, and the truck stayed with me.

In the third incident, Fred showed up at the store, saying he needed to borrow the truck again. I reluctantly gave him permission to borrow it, saying I wanted it back the next day, and as he and his girlfriend drove off, I instinctively knew something was going to happen to the truck. I had felt incredibly calm about lending him the truck. I walked back into the store five minutes later, and I heard fire engines in the distance and then driving past the store. Guess what, the truck had caught fire and burnt while he was driving it. Man, I thought that looked really good on the pair of them. Nobody was hurt, and to this day, they never did figure out what went wrong or how it caught fire. Here was an example of how my spirit friends stuck up for me. Strange things would happen all the time.

More and more I was looking for a way out of what I was into. How do you get out? I was calling out to God. Was there a God out there? Customers at the store were asking the staff if I was taking drugs because my eyes were always dilated. I must have looked strange from time to time. I am feeling more and more that something was sadly wrong with me and that I wasn't normal. I watched the movie *The Exorcist* and started reading about demons and what they can do to people. It made me sick because I felt deep down inside that there was a connection with this and my own life, but I couldn't face it yet!

On one occasion, when I was in Toronto for a gift show, there was an occult fair going on at the same time. I decided to go over and check it out. As I walked around, four different women came out of their booths and asked me to tell them their future. I had mixed feelings about this. On one hand, I felt empowered, but on the other hand, I didn't feel good about it, and I felt unclean. Something was wrong. I left and returned to the gift show.

I was still searching. I went to see a fortune-teller in the city, and out came the tarot cards. I was told that a powerful spirit was stalking me and that I was in danger. I knew this already. I had numerous spirits interacting with me, and I still also had my guardian, the big hairy nine-foot creature with whom I had picked up from the dome years ago. Unfazed by the fortune-teller's statement, I asked her what else she saw. She started to shake and asked me to bring something from my husband so she could pray over it because I was in grave danger. I thought, *I don't think so.* "Fred had left me a while ago." Then she said to me, "They are not going to let you go." I said to her, "I know that, that is nothing new." I was very frustrated because I had gone to her looking for answers, and all I saw was someone getting frightened by me. I paid her and left. Still looking for answers and because I had seen the movie *The Exorcist*, I went to see a Catholic priest, even though I am not Catholic. I started to talk to him about my life. It didn't go well. He didn't want me there. He steered me to the exit door and wanted me gone. I remember laughing at him. He was no help at all. So much for people of God assisting those who are like myself and looking for help. I was really searching at this point, and everywhere I went I seemed to be hitting closed doors.

A friend of a friend said I should make an appointment to see two Christian counselors that her friend knew, but I laughed it off, saying that I couldn't stand Christians. That was interesting because if you had asked me if I was Christian, I would have said yes because I really believed I was on the right side and serving God. This was how confused I was at the time. As I increased my search for answers, the spirits/demons began to threaten me more and more. Things were getting really tense in my life, and they said that they would also hurt or kill my two children if I carried on with this type of soul-searching. They threatened to take me out of my body again, and I would be in that black void forever. My body would be used like a zombie, a shell with something else taking over and living inside of me. I knew they could do whatever they said they could do. I was very fearful, but something inside of me said I was going in the right direction. I knew that I was going in the right direction and that I had to continue to seek the truth whatever that was.

I eventually phoned and decided to make an appointment with the two Christian counselors my friend had mentioned previously. The meeting was set. The night before the meeting, the spirits kept me awake all night, harassing and trying to intimidate yours truly. When I arrived at the couple's office, I started to talk to them about my situation in the same way I spoke to the Catholic priest, and amazingly it didn't seem to bother them. I had made up my mind that if they had started to talk about God, Jesus, or the Holy Spirit, I would be gone. Ironically, in that first meeting, they never mentioned them at all.

PART 2

Becoming a Christian

CHAPTER 13

Possession Confirmed

A rthur and Angie listened to everything that I said, and I felt that they believed me. The wife, I know now, was praying while her husband was talking and making notes. I was there about two hours and felt better after talking with them. At the end of the session, the husband handed me a sheet of paper with some instructions on it. This list detailed what I needed to start doing in order to be set free.

1. Read the book, *Inside the New Age Nightmare*, by Randall N. Baer. Publishers: Huntington House, Inc. Creation Bookstore: Ph: 659 2610. Address: 980 Oxford st. E. London, Ontario. I tried to read this book but could not. It was far too much like my life and what I was going through at the time.

2. Read the Bible. I could not get near a Bible at that time, let alone read one. It would be a long time before I would be ready to read the Bible.

Arthur also mentioned a "deliverance." I had to ask myself, what the heck was a deliverance? He also talked to me about finding a "good" Church. How would I know what a "good" Church was? So, I left that alone for a while as well.

This same piece of paper that Arthur and his wife had given to me earlier had disappeared the same night it was handed to me. I thought, *Where is God?* Suicide was looking good again. I wanted out of the life I had, God would surely understand. Suicide would stop what was happening in my body, and just maybe there would be peace at last! I didn't think Angie and Arthur had a clue how deep I was into what I was into or how far gone I was. But God did!

I knew that if I didn't follow Arthur's recommendations, then I would have gone straight to hell, no stopping on the way down. Over the next few weeks, I went for scheduled meetings with Arthur and Angie. I really didn't remember much of what was said, but I was very aware that I was doing something right. The spirits were not allowing me to sleep. I was being threatened night and day. There were times things looked three-dimensional to me, and I thought I had something wrong with my eyes. I told myself to stay on track. In my store, I had a butcher's department with all the tools. I had knives, a butcher saw, and a meat slicer—all the equipment. I was inwardly warned to stay away from this area because I sensed my spirits might cause an accident. I also had to be very careful when I drove my car anywhere.

Again I cried out, "What about my children? What have they done to deserve all this?" A voice within me said, *They are protected no matter how the spirits threaten you. Your children are safe.* What could I do, I just had to believe, let it go, and keep going forward. I was one little minnow in a very big pond. I asked the spirits, "Why was all this happening to me, all this 'spiritual' stuff? Why did my spirits think I was so important as to create so much havoc in my life?" I should not have asked this question.

I had met a man through a friend of mine named Alex. He invited me to visit his sister's place. She lived just outside of London in a small town. Alex liked to drink. I told him that if he was driving, there would be no drinking. It was a very pleasant evening. I kept a watchful eye on Alex, and as far as I could see, he was as good as his word and didn't touch a drop of alcohol. We said our good-byes to his sister around midnight, but just before this, I was starting to feel very uneasy. I had a premonition that something was going to happen and that it wasn't good. I even accused Alex of drinking when I wasn't looking, and he assured me that he had not. We got in the car, and I was still feeling very uneasy about everything. Alex looked at me and grinned. The man looking at me was not Alex; even though it looked like Alex, it wasn't him. We were now on the main highway, two lanes each side, and there was a fair bit of traffic even for that time of night.

Alex spoke to me, but his voice was different. "You are special, we need you back. Too much training has been put into you. You are not your own, but you are ours." This particular spirit had kicked Alex out of his body and now was using it for its own purposes. Something else was using it. I froze within myself. I locked myself within myself. Within me, a voice said, *Call it Alex and no other name.* I spoke and called it Alex, and that it did not like. It promptly accelerated the car, looking at me while driving far too fast, and I thought we were going to crash into the cars driving on the other side lane. The car was swerving in and out of the traffic. I couldn't believe that no one had yet called the police. This was craziness. His behavior was wild but strangely controlled. It (the demon) had the upper hand and said it was time I knew my place and that they were going to do whatever they needed to do to scare me into submission. I had no idea where we were, and I remained frozen. Silently, I cried, "Somebody help me, please."

I do remember saying to Alex, "I told you not to drink, and what you are doing now is not funny." Almost immediately, "it" sharply took a turn off of the highway, which turned into a country lane. It said to me, "Look what I can do. I am Jesus." Before my eyes, a fog came out of nowhere, a very thick fog. It was looking right at me, grinning, oozing evil, and it smelled horrible. "I am your Jesus," it said and then put its foot down on the accelerator, and we drove right into the thick fog. With the wave of its hand, the fog was gone. As for me, I was wishing I was gone, but this "thing" was still beside me.

Suddenly, I just knew Alex's body had to go to the bathroom! It stopped the car. Meanwhile, I am thinking, "You stop and get out, and I am moving over to the driver's seat, and I am gone!" I didn't care if I was leaving it or Alex behind. But just as the car stopped, it leaned over to me, laughed, and pulled the keys out. It left the car to relieve Alex's body. I was in shock. It had no problem reading my mind, and I had no problem reading it. What was I to do now? This was hell on earth!

It (Alex) got back in the car and drove, and I said, "Alex, you must be tired. Let me drive." It then proceeded to demoralize women, and I was included. It absolutely, totally, and completely hated women. Alex would come back from time to time, sounding drunk, and then "it" would come back into him again. This happened over and over. At long last, the car stopped, and Alex was back. I said, "I will drive," so we switched places. When I was behind the wheel, I had no idea where I was or how to get back home. Alex looked like he had fallen asleep in the time we switched places—no, passed out was more like it. I had started to drive. After a while, I saw lights of a city in the distance, so I drove towards the lights. Alex's body would wake up periodically, go on again about women, putting them and me down, and then calm down, and I would see Alex asleep. This went on back and forth while I was driving back to the city. I thought, *Tomorrow is another day, and tonight is still not over. Help! Help! Help!*

I knew I had to stay awake and keep my wits about me. Alex, at some point, took over driving again. I think this time I passed out. I wanted to stay awake and alert. I actually came too as he pulled up outside his apartment. He said, "You can sleep in my room, and I'll take you home in the morning." I was not myself, but I knew what was going on. I kept checking that it was Alex and not the other thing. Everything seemed okay until we got inside his apartment. I went into the bedroom, and he followed. I reminded him that he was sleeping in the living room on the couch. I have the bedroom. He had dropped the keys down on a table just inside the door. When he wasn't looking, I whipped them up and hid them on my person. I got into bed fully clothed and waited till he went to sleep. My plan was that once he was asleep, I would be gone. What was the time? We left his sister's house at midnight, and God only knows what time it was now. Would I be sane the next day? Who would care, anyway?

As I write this, a scripture came to mind, which I need to share with you now.

"Even though I walk through the valley of the shadow of death, I will fear no evil, for you are with me; your rod and your staff, they comfort me." (Psalm 23:4).

I cried out deep from within my being, "If there is a God up there, please help me!"

I had left the bedroom door open a crack, and I could hear him talking to himself. Evil surrounded me, I had no room to move, and I could smell it. It smelled like death. All went quiet. Good, I thought, and then all of a sudden, I instinctively knew it was back. I heard it get up. I thought my number was up, and I wondered if it was coming into the bedroom. The phone rang, it stopped coming toward the bedroom door, went back to the couch, and picked the phone up. I was paralyzed with fear. It or they had already threatened to rip me apart, what could happen now?

It was speaking in a deep, guttural voice that dripped evil. It was the most unholy, unclean conversation about women and myself that I had ever heard. And what it thought of me was beyond belief. It was so extreme. I just knew I was in trouble! I had no idea how to get out, but I did have the car keys. So, why was I still alive? Who was it talking to on the phone? Was it talking to another demon? I had no idea. It was a hotline to hell as far as I was concerned. I just tried to stay calm. I heard the phone go down and then silence. Then Alex was asleep, snoring.

Again, I heard an inner voice, *Gloria, leave nothing behind that belongs to you. Take it with you. You are safe, he will not wake up.* Somehow, I knew that was true. I checked for my things, a couple of books, etc. I had the keys and crept out down to the car. I prayed it would start first time, and it did. I left, driving slowly, and the further away from that place I got, the lighter I felt. Literally tons of evil were being released from me and letting me go. I was no longer afraid, and I was just driving slowly back home to the store, and I was so thankful I was still alive and in my right mind. It was seven in the morning when I arrived back. I parked the car and left the day shift a note to give Alex his keys back and to tell him that they had no idea where I was. I went up to my apartment and crashed.

I heard from the girls who worked for me in the store say a few days later that Alex had tried to smash his car into a tree. He told the girls that on that night, he felt he had been raped and was trying to get back into his body. He even went to see his doctor because he felt so ill and out of it. I thought, *Alex, you are on your own. I am trying to survive too. I don't even want to talk to you.* My girls wanted me to talk to him because Alex was coming into the store regularly, asking for me. But I didn't want to talk to him. It didn't seem to matter whom I got involved with, my spirits would get into their bodies. What was in me could enter anyone's body at will.

A few days later, the girls working for me at the store showed me an article in the local paper about the house right next to Alex's apartment. Evidently, there was a man living there who suffered from depression. He had hung himself sometime in the night, the same night I was there at Alex's apartment. There was pure evil all around Alex's place that night. I felt responsible for Alex and for the man who hung himself, and these things stayed with me for a long time. Who was responsible for me?

Psalm 23:3 says, "(Jesus) He restores my soul."

I ask you, did I need to take drugs to take trips? No! And unless you can say you have walked in my shoes, do not judge or condemn me. After my deliverance, I asked God, "Why did you bother with me?" He replied, "My grace, my child, my grace." I was going to weekly meetings with the Christian counselors. I see now they were very good for me and that it was a very safe place for me. I still had upsets, but I still kept forging ahead. My life couldn't get much worse, yet I had nothing to lose, just my soul; the spirits were not getting that without a fight.

At one of the meetings with my counselors, Arthur was going on about demon possession or something along those lines. I asked God, "If you are there, I need to know if I have anything inside of me that should not be there." The very next week, there I was again at their house and office; their dog was so pleased to see me. We were in the office, and Arthur was talking about Jesus. I started to feel quite sick. (At the time, I didn't associate feeling sick with the name of Jesus.) The feeling didn't go away, and then I was feeling faint. It kept getting worse. His wife asked me if I needed air. "Are you all right?" she asked. I said yes but that I needed air, and so I went out into the back garden. Their spoiled dog came with me. It was dark outside. My stomach was churning, I was physically sick, and I was cold and clammy. The dog was beside me but then suddenly gone. I stood up and noticed he was up against the back door. Every hair on his body was standing on end, his eyes wide open. He was growling and whining and showing his teeth all while he was looking right at me. At the same time, he was banging his body against the screen door. Arthur came up to see what all the noise was about. The dog flew into the house, not to be seen again that night.

What did the dog see in me? He was obviously not liking what he saw, and there was great fear in his eyes. I was seeing a missing link. What had been my question the week before—"Show me if I have anything unclean within me." I guess the question had been answered. I went back to the office and sat down. Immediately, my temperature went up, and I broke out in welts all over my body. Inside of me, a battle was raging. The battle was good against evil. I curled up in a ball in pain and shouted to Arthur and Angie, "Don't touch me! I could contaminate you. I am impure." I know they didn't touch me, but I bet they were praying. Life goes on. I have spent all the years of my life so far under the control of the spirits' inside of me, but this was going to end; change was in the wind. I knew this for sure.

Somewhere in all this mess, Fred and I were getting a divorce. There were problems with how our money and possessions were to be divided. Three lawyers, Fred, and myself met in one of their offices to sort this out and not go to court. As I was driving to the meeting, a surge of rejection and loneliness and feeling of being unloved and unwanted all came at me. I called out again, "God, are you there?' Here comes the voice again from within, different from all the other voices. It warned me that I could not keep the dome. I had to release it. Within me, I knew that this was right. The argument started in the lawyer's office when Fred stated he did not want the dome. "You would die for that dome," he said, "so pay me, and it is yours." How true, I would have died for that ninety-seven acres of land and the dome not too long ago, but now here was a voice telling me to disconnect from all this. It wasn't for me anymore, and I knew it. If I kept the dome, all that I have in me (my spirits) would stay because I would have been giving them permission to stay by keeping the dome and the land it sat on. I ask you, why was my life so problematic?

The afternoon in the lawyer's office rolled on. Nothing was getting resolved, and I was not taking the dome or the land it sat on. Then suddenly, the atmosphere started changing within the office. I looked at everybody, but nobody sensed anything. Then Fred spoke, but it was not his voice. I looked at the lawyers and wondered why they didn't see that it was not Fred anymore. Here we go again. A powerful spirit/demon entered into Fred, which I thought at the time might have even been satan. It was angry, and its anger was directed straight at me. By saying that I was not taking the dome or the land it sat on, I was totally disconnecting from the evil supernatural forces that were in my life. The thing in Fred was furious. It called me a witch and more right there in the lawyer's office. I was not looking at the lawyers' faces here. It told me that I would regret all I had put it (Fred) through. It told me, "You had better take the dome and look after it as you should!" Here was another mega spiritual battle going on.

Now here's another shocker. I was looking at the lawyers, and they had seemed to not hear a word. It was as if there was a smoke screen or a veil that had been put up between Fred, myself, and them. Fred's face had even changed. If looks could kill, I should have died right there on the spot. Action! Confronting it was not on my menu. *I am undone*, I cried out within myself. I was scared silly. I told the lawyers I was going to the washroom. I sat on the toilet and cried out, "What am I going to do now?" I heard a voice, and it had to have been God and only God. It said, *My child, you will go back in there, and this is exactly what you will say. "Fred, you can keep your tattoo business, the land, the dome, and everything connected with it. On top of this, I will give you fifty thousand dollars. I will keep the store and everything connected with it. You have only twenty minutes to make up your mind. If you do not agree, then we will go to court.*"

I was still sitting on the toilet. I slowly digested what was said, calmed down, left the washroom, and walked back to the lawyer's office. I walked up to Fred (it was still not him) and repeated everything that I had been told to say by God, looking boldly right into his (its) eyes. Where did my strength come from? It came from my God whom I didn't even know properly as yet. He knew me and was making a straight path for me against all odds.

The lawyer's office went quiet after what I had said; we were all waiting for Fred to make up his mind. I must be honest, I didn't think that he was going to go for the offer I had been instructed to lay on the table. But at the last minute, what was in him said, "I agree to it." The time was 5.20 p.m., I remember it well. My lawyer was furious with me. "I was out of line," she said afterwards with the way I had handled my offer. My reaction to this came easy. I said, "I needed my husband and you out of my life so I could get on with my life." Only God could have gotten me through all that had happened. There were seven people in that office that day, not five—God and Gloria, Fred, satan, and three lawyers—and who won the day? God and Gloria. God will always have the last word. His Word is the law, and everything will bow their knee.

The land and the dome had now been unloaded in one move. Was I making progress? Yes! And with lots of help from God, whom I was developing a relationship with. This was one huge spiritual battle that had just unfolded in Fred's lawyer's office. As my relationship with the Lord developed, He showed me how in the future I would be able to capture my enemies (the demons), and I will throw them into a flaming furnace, and the Lord will consume them in His anger. He will protect me, and He will turn the tables on them. I will be there to watch the demons that controlled me be defeated.

"You will capture all your enemies. Your strong right hand will seize all who hate you. You will throw them into a flaming furnace when you appear. The LORD will consume them in his anger; fire will devour them. You will wipe their children from the face of the earth; they will never have descendants. Although they plot against you, their evil schemes will never succeed. For they will turn and run when they see your arrows aimed at them. Rise up, O LORD in all you power. With music and singing we celebrate your mighty acts" (Psalm 21:8–13, Life Applications Study Bible).

"The Lord is my strength and shield. I trust him with all my heart. He helps me, and my heart is filled with joy. I burst out in songs of thanksgiving" (Psalm 28:7, Life Application Study Bible).

CHAPTER 14

God Is in Control of My House

What was in me knew what was happening, and I became more harassed, inflicted, and tormented as my deliverance date drew nearer. A battle was raging inside of me. I knew I was on the right path, but I didn't know if I would be alive or dead or sane at the end of it. The end of May was the date set at the church for my deliverance. I was in such a state and suspicious of everyone and everything seen and not seen. I was even hallucinating. I felt as though I was high on drugs and the spirits were pushing all of my buttons. I was seeing double, I looked spaced out, and people thought I was on drugs. It really was a spiritual battle. If at any time I had committed suicide or had an accident or taken my life, I would have gone straight to hell. It was better for the spirits if I had died before I was delivered. Continuous pressure was exerted on me, and I felt that so intensely. "Don't let me die, God!" I cried. "Not like this."

I was told that thirty-three people were praying for me daily at the church. That meant absolutely *nothing* to me. I didn't want the demons to take over my body anymore or send me insane, and I was still worried about what was going to happen to my two children. I told Arthur that due to the severity of the attacks both spiritually and physically (not sure whether he believed me or not), the deliverance had to be *now*! I knew I would not last another week. My machinery in the store was acting up, and it would stop working when I was cutting meat and then start up again when I was trying to fix it. Also, they would not let me sleep. I was exhausted and run-down, so instead of being delivered end of May, it was put forward to May fourth, a Friday.

On Wednesday night Arthur told me that I had to get rid of all my spiritual paraphernalia before my deliverance, which was happening Friday. They all had to be destroyed, including books. Why? The Lord God would deliver me, but the spirits would see what I still had in my possession and come back with a vengeance. The house would not have been swept clean. I would then be in a worse state than I was before. Was that possible? Yes. Everything that had come from them had to be destroyed. Here is a list of some of these articles that had to be destroyed: a sword, picture of a wolf, New Age books, Tibetan bells, statues of dragons, candles, jewelry (including certain pieces left to me by my grandmother and my mother), incense and holders, crystals, semiprecious stones, artifacts, personal notes of my training, peacock feathers, and certain clothing.

I had to burn a particular "robe" that was given to me as a gift. Why? Because I was wearing it when I was praying against the enemy as led by the spirits (but really I was praying against Christians). When I asked God why I had to burn this particular robe, He gave me this scripture: "Snatch others from the fire and save them; to others show mercy mixed with fear – hating even the *clothing* stained by corrupted flesh" (Jude2:22). My flesh was corrupted because of what I did when I was wearing this robe against my flesh.

I didn't argue with Arthur about any of the "stuff" I was to get rid of. It was like I had God's compass within me, a magnetic needle that was pointing me in the right direction. Arthur finished off by saying, "If you don't destroy this evil garbage, please do not bother coming on Friday because you will be wasting God's time. The demons will just come back, but this time with even more of them." Now we are at Thursday, the day before the deliverance. The pastor and his wife who had taken me under their wing thought it would be a good idea for me to spend Friday during the day with them.

Everybody at the church was still praying for me, thirty-three people plus those I have previously mentioned. The pastor felt I would be in a safe environment with him and his wife.

Thursday evening, the night before the deliverance, about eight o'clock, I was working in the store with two other staff members. My part-time butcher was there cutting the meat for roasts. We closed at ten. Remember, I could talk to the spirits/demons with my mind just like I talk with a human being. I still had not had time to get rid of all my spiritually evil garbage. I told the spirits that once the store was closed, a spring cleaning was going to take place. I would be dispersing and burning everything connected with them. *Very brave, Gloria!*

Next thing I know, as I went back to the meat counter to talk to the butcher, I was walking down the aisle, as I approached the butcher counter, I was pushed from the right side so hard I went straight down onto my left side. *Bang!* I hit the cement floor! The glass ornament I had in my hand fell, hit the floor, broke, and cut me over my eyebrow. Somehow, I twisted my left knee, and I also fell directly on my left arm and side. My arm was fractured, but I didn't know it at the time. All the wind was knocked out of me, and I couldn't get my breath.

Nobody else but the three of us were in the store. Nobody was near me, so who pushed me? You are only allowed one guess, and you are right—it was them. I heard Roy call to Linda, "Where did Gloria go?" He came around the counter, and there I was winded lying on the floor. They both helped me up. I then worked till ten in the evening and closed the store in my injured state. My mind was reeling, when does this all stop? Then with the help of a friend, I burnt, smashed, ripped apart, put into garbage bags, mixed with rotten waste that was going to the dump, all that evil disgusting stuff I used to value so highly. Before this, I would have guarded it with my life, and now I couldn't wait to unload it. I didn't want anyone else to find this stuff and be able to use it or keep this evil garbage in their possession. It was now two thirty early morning, and I then went to the local hospital to have my arm fixed. They asked me how the accident happened, and I just told them I tripped and fell (that was sort of true). I had no sleep that night, and I didn't know what was going to happen to me next. I was so drained. I was past being scared; it was as if I was shell shocked, and nobody was home.

It is now Friday morning, and my staff were in charge of the store for the next week. With my arm in a sling, a cut above my eye, and limping, I went to the pastor's house. I have no idea what I did or said or anything. I wondered how I still managed to be alive. The pastor's wife thought it would be a good idea for me to get some fresh air. When we went outside, we were nearly run down by a car at a pedestrian crossing. She quickly took me back to their house. Nothing was said about this.

I arrived at the church around seven in the evening, and my daughter met us there, along with all the people there to help with my deliverance. The deliverance group involved six people whom Arthur and Angie had arranged to pray for me plus the thirty-three other people in the church who had been praying for me for some time. Forgive me if I sound sarcastic, but I was so thankful to anyone whom God had used to get me to the right side!

How do I repay God for what He did for me and the people who were so obedient to Him? How great is His love for the lost. Remember I was not yet a Christian, and I had unknowingly prayed against Christians in the past. Amazingly, just like the one lost sheep that went missing in the Bible, the flock was safe, but the little sheep wasn't, and so Jesus came to find her. Luke 15:4 says, "If a man has a hundred sheep and one of them gets lost, what will he do? Won't he leave the ninety-nine others in the wilderness and go to search for the one that is lost until he finds it?"

As I am writing this, I am trying to fathom why God saved me, especially when I think of Job. Job is an interesting character in the Bible. He was tested, and he is portrayed as a wealthy man of upright character who loves God, yet God allowed satan to destroy his flocks, possessions, children, and his health, but satan could not take his life. And through all of this, Job refused to give up on God, even though he didn't understand why all these bad things were happening to him (Job 1:1, Life Applications Study Bible). God alone knew the purpose behind Job's suffering, and He never explained it to Job. Yet still Job focused on God alone. So, why was God saving me after

I lived so uncleanly, and yet someone as holy as Job had to endure such hardship? I don't know why one person who is righteous and who loves God has to endure hardship while somebody like myself has sinned and been into all kinds of unholy things, yet God gave me grace and would not allow the enemy to maim or destroy me. It is obviously not our place to judge what or why God does things the way he does.

I must confess that a year after my deliverance, I was very angry at God. I said to God, "Why didn't you rescue me and restore me when I was twenty, thirty, or forty years old? Why did you wait until I was fifty? Was I someone's guinea pig again? God worked through this with me. The Lord finally brought me through my dilemma of why He didn't save me when I was younger. But just like Job, I had to work my way through all of my misgivings. The Lord guided me in believing that I had to focus on what He was doing in my life now and let go of what had happened before. The sooner I let go of the past, the sooner I could heal and get on with my life the way the Lord had planned for me.

Who can claim to know and understand God's purpose in their lives? It certainly was not me! At the same time, the Lord gave me a vision of this absolutely magnificent lion who was holding a very large and unruly cub by the scruff of its neck. The lion was dragging the cub along, making sure the cub was going to where He needed it to go. I laughed when the Lord showed me this, and I thought it was funny. God said to me, "Why are you laughing, my child? That cub is you." That melted me from the inside out.

Back to the Friday deliverance night at the church. It was to be done downstairs in the offices of the church. My daughter was in the room with me. Six people were watching me and praying. I wondered to myself if the people in the room thought I might foam at the mouth, roll on the floor screaming, take the form of a snake, or something worse during the deliverance. I had no idea what was inside of me, what it would do, or how the other people might react to this. I just wanted to remain sane and for all parts of me (soul and spirit) to remain attached to me. If the deliverance was a success, there would be no more kicking me out of my body and throwing me into a black void. No more separations of mind, body, soul, and spirit.

My daughter and I arrived at the church with Arthur and Angie. We went downstairs to an office. My mind was not clear as I looked through my eyes; there was a haze in the room. Everyone there was deep in prayer with their eyes open, watching me. First, there was a prayer, and then Arthur started to renounce under the guidance of the Holy Spirit the spirits of hell that had been in my life. One by one, I had to repeat what was said, I remember thinking you don't give them names because that gives them power. A voice within said, *Gloria, just repeat what Arthur is saying.* So I did as I was told. I was submitting and renouncing out loud everything Arthur said, whether I agreed with it or not.

I really don't remember what followed after that; to me it went on and on for what seemed like an infinite amount of time. I didn't feel good. I sensed a heaviness that seemed to have invaded the room. I was feeling very hot, and I was uncomfortable. What was coming? Here it comes. Arthur asked me, "Will I accept Jesus Christ as my Lord and savior?" He then said, "By the blood of Jesus, I would be saved." I do not remember the words exactly as Arthur spoke them, but I certainly remember the content. I instantly felt panic, panic panic! How could I say these words? I didn't believe in Jesus Christ. I had been taught by the spirits that Jesus was just a low prophet. I didn't love Jesus, I didn't know him, and I didn't know much about him at all, so how could I say I loved him? How could I repeat what Arthur was saying? I felt it would have been a lie. I worried that the spirits that were still controlling my life would know I was lying, and even though there was a deliverance taking place, I would not be telling the truth, so they could still come back again. That is what I believed at the time.

Arthur was waiting for me to repeat the words and receive Christ. I was panicking and cried out within myself, *Help me! I don't want to go back to those spirits ever!* A voice answered me, and I knew it was God the Father. *My child, say the words, come across, and you will learn to love my Son.* I knew in that moment that things would work out for me no matter how bad it all looked now. My children would be safe, for God would be watching over all of us. Then I repeated the words I was asked to repeat with no problem. I immediately felt that something had left me. It was like turning a light switch on, just like that. I didn't foam at the mouth or squirm on the floor in epileptic convulsions. It was done; I was delivered. Here was my new beginning. I was delivered from a legion of demons all at once, and I had no idea how long the process took. My daughter to this day remembers very little about what took place, even though she was there with me. Angie thought it would be good if I went upstairs and thanked all the people who had prayed for me. I was feeling very weak, but I did what she asked and went upstairs. I was still not fully understanding all of what had happened to me just a short while ago. It was all too much to take in.

Weeks later, I went to a healing and deliverance service. Here the Holy Spirit baptized me in fire, and for the first time I spoke in tongues. Then came more tutoring, and later on I was baptized by water in the church. Here God spoke to my heart. "Tell all assembled here, child, here is one that I, God, have brought back from the pit of hell." This I did with joy in my heart.

Much later in my Christian walk, I struggled with my Father's words, which he had shared with me on that night. "Come across, my child, and you will learn to love my Son." I have come to love and honor Jesus in worship and many other ways just as God said, so it became real in my life. Then God gave me the following scriptures. "Then (Jesus said), that is why I said that people can't come to me *unless the Father gives them to me*" (John 6:65, Life Applications Study Bible). This is what my heavenly Father did for me in that room at that church years ago. It was a miracle and what a revelation for me. God gave me to his son Jesus Christ on that day, May 4, 1989. I was delivered and set free from demons. That gift was given to me so undeserved yet so lovingly given. How great is our God; He overruled satan and his demons, and they could do nothing about God's decision. I was set free from them.

The second scripture that God gave me was John 14:6, "Jesus told him (Thomas) I am the way, the truth, and the life. *No one can come to the Father except through Me.*" Here God was showing me again that Jesus is the way, He is both God and man. By giving my life to Him, I was also giving my life to God, my Father, and the Holy Spirit. I pray this helps others who are struggling to find the right "path." Both of my children now had the curse broken off of them. Just think about this—had I died before my deliverance, my daughter would have inherited all that evil I had within me, and the curse would have continued on. But it was *stopped* by God, and satan could do nothing to stop this from happening. Praise You, Father. Both my children were now free from any unholy alliances, free to make good choices.

The following day after my deliverance, I went back to the store, picked up my bags, and a friend and I went to the States. No one could contact me, and it was a complete break for me. Before I came back to my new life at the store as a new believer in Christ, my mind was still very much mixed up, my body felt bruised, but the miracle was that I was altogether spiritually in one body. It would still take me some time, however, before I would feel fully complete. I had no energy, I felt as if I had been beaten within an inch of my life, my arm was still sore, and I was still limping from the night I eliminated all my unholy spiritual paraphernalia. I was still very much a mess, but I did feel some comfort in knowing I was altogether in my body with no more separations. The fact that I was delivered still meant very little to me. I was not hearing my voices anymore. And I was so glad I had arranged to have a week off from work with my friend far away from everything.

Read Mark 5:1–20: "For Jesus had already said to the spirit, 'Come out of the man you evil spirit.' Then Jesus demanded, 'What is you name?' and he replied, 'My name is legion, because there are many of us inside this man...'"

When I returned from the States, I was told by Arthur and Angie that I must start going to church. They explained that I needed to have fellowship with Christians, but they also told me to not talk about my recent past. It was better not to revisit it with people who were meeting me for the first time. Question: why wouldn't the people rejoice that God had set me free? I also had to read and study my Bible. All of this was necessary for me to keep my freedom in

Christ. Obviously, the battle was still on, so even though I had been delivered, I was still seeing demons (although they were not able to reside in my body anymore). The spirits were now trying to make me believe that I had not been saved and that I still belonged to them!

My transition to being a Christian was painfully slow and difficult. I was still seeing the demons, still hearing things in my store, even though I was now Christian. The process was tedious. In the meantime, I was also becoming more aware of the reality that I was a store owner who employed people and that it was my livelihood. There were no voices to give me advice anymore and no voices to give me direction. I was slowly becoming shockingly aware of just how much the spirits guided and directed every aspect of my life. So now it was like being a six-year-old who had a business that I owned but was having difficulty on how to run it.

I was like a completely new person coming at my life in a whole new way. I was an empty husk after my deliverance. I had to get reacquainted with my life and with me. Did I want this? No! I really wanted my life to be smooth sailing. When you have spirits directing your life from within you your entire life until you are fifty, and then suddenly they are gone and you are now clean, you need to learn how to walk again a different way; this was not quite what I had expected. At that time, I remember hiding in my apartment as much as I could. This new life was not easy for me, and I felt out of my depth. I would spend Sundays pouring over my business paperwork, trying to figure out what was going on with me and my business so that come Monday, I looked like I knew what I was doing. I was, however, quite sure that the Lord would fill this gap that I felt within me, but I still had to contend with everything that was coming at me in a normal everyday way as a single woman who owned and operated a relatively successful business and was only just now realizing what I was into it in a new way. Now I was all me. I wasn't being guided by voices anymore. As good as all that was, I was terrified, and I thought I was going to go mad again! So much for thatched cottages and roses round the door. Ha-ha! I went from one horrendous experience into another.

Reading the Bible was a struggle. I could touch and turn the pages, but I could still not read it. A deacon in a church I visited with a friend was trying to help me with reading my Bible. Although he was trying to be helpful, he was being quite controlling about what I should do and how I should do it. Every time he saw me over the next few weeks, he kept telling me the same thing. In the end, I told him to back off. I had no idea why I couldn't read the Bible, and I told this deacon that God would guide me when I was ready. God had delivered me, so He certainly would know when I was ready to read my Bible, right?

What did deliverance actually mean to me?

- no more demonic control

- no more evil influences

- no more bewitchments, sorcery, spells, psychic powers, and evil influences, which had been running though my family line for generations

- freedom from all curses placed upon our family line, which, if they had not been stopped by God, would have carried on into future generations

- freedom from slavery and spiritual torture

- the ability to make right and sound decisions for the rest of my life under the stewardship of God

- no more nervous breakdowns, sleepless nights, and always being emotionally disturbed

- no more demons using my mind, body, and spirit for their own evil ends

I ask you, what did I have to lose by changing sides? Giving myself to God, Jesus Christ, and the Holy Spirit—I call this a win-win situation despite all the problems. Again, I thank God for all his grace and mercy in my tiny complex life. Isaiah 8:19 says, "Someone may say to you, 'Let's ask the mediums and those who consult the spirits of the dead. With their whisperings and mutterings, they will tell us what to do." But shouldn't people ask God for guidance? Should the living seek guidance from the dead? *Never*! See 1 Samuel 28, the whole chapter, "King Saul Consults a Medium." It took about nine months before I could actually start to read the Bible. One day, the Holy Spirit came upon me, and we read the whole book of Hebrews together. It was awesome! From then on, I was free to read the Bible. I actually understood what I was reading, and it came alive for me. It made sense to me. It showed me that Christ is the high priest in the New Testament and that He is greater than the angels because He is God's own son. I read from chapter 1 right through to chapter 13.

Hebrews 13:20 reads, "Now may the God of peace – who brought up from the dead our Lord Jesus, the great Shepherd of the sheep, and ratified an eternal covenant with his blood – may He equip you with all you need for doing His will. May He produce in you, through the power of Jesus Christ, every good thing that is pleasing to Him. All glory to Him forever and ever! Amen."

This gave me a hunger for the rest of the Bible.

The next big thing for me was to find a church to go to. If you have not ever gone to church before, how do you know a good church from a bad church? I was told to go to a "good" Bible-based church, but being totally new to Christianity, I had no idea what that meant. My thought on this was to go to the same one that Arthur and Angie went to, that would be a start. Another couple who were also a pastor and wife team, did a lot to mentor and disciple me in those early days. They all went to the same church. I remember holding onto the pew in front of me, so I wouldn't leave. I saw demons walking about in the church like they owned the place. Some of these demons looked disgusting, some looked like stick figures. I didn't like to dwell on them; they did not all look the same, they were clearly not of this world. I thought, if this was God's church, what were they doing here? We were all under the same roof—demons, God, Holy Spirit, Jesus, and the people. Were we all on the same side with no dividing line, all mashed up together in the same pot? This was really confusing to me. Later on, it came to me that the demons were there because of the sin in people's lives.

One day, I went up to the front of the church for an altar call. While one of the people on the ministry team prayed for me, something was also attacking me, trying to pull the hair from my head. Was the church unclean? I asked myself. Where do I fit in? I was surprised that no one else seemed to be able to sense or see what I saw. Christians told me that Christians do not have demons in them. I reported these things to those in authority in the church, about what I was seeing. They did not like me talking about this and doubted what I was saying, so I ended up keeping my own counsel. "God," I cried out, "why do I have to go to church? I don't like it and I didn't fit in." I was just an outsider looking in, and I was so uncomfortable with what I was seeing. How do you explain as you watch in church a demon getting your attention and then going and kissing a deacon on the cheek? Then it turns, looks at you, and grins. I didn't know what sin that particular man had been into, but I could get that it wasn't entirely holy. When I saw this, I would pray, "Dear Lord, help him and help me. Amen." My prayer for the deacon was very short and sweet, as I really didn't know how to pray, but felt my prayer would suffice.

Here I had just been saved spiritually, and now I am in another kind of mindfield. The Lord answered all my questions, but I asked again and again, why do I have to go back to church? Back would come the same answer, "Obedience, my child."

Arthur and Angie were not counseling me anymore. They felt that their job was done. Maybe it was. I felt at the time that their job was far from finished. There were times when I was straight out vulnerable to anything spiritual. The demons were still saying that I was theirs. Carefully, I would approach the counselors, Arthur and Angie, about certain situations, and the response was always, "We are busy, you are fine, get on with your life now." I thought, *Okay, I have come out of the occult, and what a battle that was, so why am I still having so many battles now?* It was a great relief to me years later when I read a booklet entitled *The Facts on the Occult* by J. Ankerberg and J. Weldon. The pages in this book stood out like a neon sign smacking me in the face with the truth. I agreed with what these authors said in their book. How many times did the battles rage around me with me doubting whether I was really saved or not? How afraid and scared I was that the demons would take me back. My saving graces were God Himself never letting me go, Jesus always standing in the gap for me, and the Holy Spirit guiding and counselling me through all of these turbulent times. I asked myself, how many souls had been saved and then lost because of a lack of knowledge and discipleship? So few supposed experts really know how to handle these types of spiritual battles.

Our true counselor must be the Holy Spirit, and if any person or Christian is supporting, counseling, coaching anyone who has been involved with any type of demonic activity either knowingly or not, it is best not to get involved unless you are led completely by the Holy Spirit. To know for sure whether or not you are being led by the Holy Spirit would, in my experience, require several days of deep prayer, waiting to be guided appropriately by the Lord. Too many times individuals get involved in things they should leave well alone. A good guideline is taken from the book *The Facts on the Occult* by J Ankerberg and J. Weldon (pp.37-43).

First and foremost, a correct diagnosis is essential! for example, mental illness must not be mistaken for occult bondage. A person must truly be experiencing demonic oppression from real occult activities; otherwise, misdiagnosis can cause serious problems.

Second, it must be recognized that a genuine battle is in progress. A very real enemy has been encountered, and this enemy is dangerous. But it must also be realized that Christ has obtained victory. Because a real battle has been engaged, Dr. Koch cautions that people are not to rush into the area of occult counseling. Rather, they should seriously look to God for a leading in this area. Spiritual maturity and spiritual insight are vital:

Third, we need to recognize God's sovereignty. Christ and Christ alone is the source of deliverance. The usual procedures—psychology, ritual hypnosis, meditation, etc.—are useless and may compound the problem. Further, God does not require our "often complicated counseling procedures." However, deliverance without any counseling at all is rare. Also full deliverance may take weeks, months, or sometimes years; or by God's sovereignty it may require only a few hours.

"Fourth, all paraphernalia of occultism must be destroyed (Acts 19:19). "Magical books and occult objects carry with them a hidden ban. Anyone not prepared to rid himself of this ban will be unable to free himself from the influence of the powers of darkness" (p.90)…"

"In addition, all occult contacts and friendships must be broken and not even gifts from occultists should be accepted. In a difficult case of a saved person living with parents who are occultists, it may even be necessary for them to secure other living arrangements.…"

"Fifth, deliverance from the power of the occult requires complete surrender to Christ on the part of both counselor and counselee.… Every person who really wants to be delivered from the hold of the occult must be prepared to commit his life entirely to Christ.… If Jesus Christ Himself is truly our Lord, then He will protect us from the lordship of others; but if our commitment is half-hearted, we may be asking for unnecessary problems."

"Sixth, the occultly oppressed person must acknowledge and confess his participation in occult activity as sin, because such practices are sinful before God and require confession (Deuteronomy 18:9-12; 1 John 1:9). In addition, confession must be voluntary, or it is worthless.… Every sin connected with sorcery is basically a contract with the powers of darkness. By means of sorcery, the arch enemy of mankind gains the right of ownership over a person's life. The same is true even if it is only the sins of a person's parents or grandparents that are involved. The devil is well acquainted with the second commandment which ends, "for I the Lord your God am a jealous God, visiting the iniquity of the fathers upon the children to the third and the fourth generation of those who hate me".

"Seventh, it is vital to assure the individual that in Christ his sins have been forgiven, and that he now possesses an eternal salvation that cannot be taken from him. No matter how bad a person's sins may have been, they have been forgiven. Appropriate Scripture passages may be read such as John 5:24; 6:47; 19:30; Romans 5:20; Galatians 1:4; Ephesians 1:7, 13, 14; Colossians 1:14; 1 Peter 1:3-5, 18, 19; Hebrews 1:3; Isiah 53: 4-7; 1 Peter 2:24; 1 John 1:7-9; etc."

"It is also to be recognized that counseling should involve teamwork. The support of other Christians, church elders, etc. is important. As Koch explains, "Counseling the occultly oppressed is really a matter of teamwork. The individual counselor is far too weak to take upon his own shoulders all the problems he meets. For example, people with occult subjection will often suffer their first attacks after they seek to follow Christ and serve Him. In other words, the battle often does not begin until a person receives Christ…"

"Eighth, prayer is another critical aspect of counseling. People who are delivered from the occult are still vulnerable even after being delivered. It is thus vital that a small group of Christians take upon themselves to continue to pray for them and care for them after their conversion. Sometimes Christians do not recognise how important this is. Many converted occultists have struggled tremendously because they could find no one in the church to help them….

"No matter how difficult or how wearying the counseling of occultly oppressed people may be, the truth remains that the victory is won because of what Christ has accomplished. Counselors need to believe God's promises and act in faith even in what seem to be hopeless situations. No situation is finally hopeless, for with God all things are possible…. True deliverance will never be forthcoming in an unscriptural atmosphere – even if the battle for the oppressed person appears to be very dramatic. We must be on our guard against every kind of excess, and above all against exhibitionism. Let us therefore be: Sound in our faith, Sober in our thoughts, Honest and scriptural in our attitude."

A scripture comes to mind, which I like to share with you now. Luke 11:21–22 says, "For when a strong man like satan is fully armed and guards his palace, his possessions are safe until someone even stronger attacks and overpowers him, strips him of his weapons and carries off his belongings." So satan had me and my life inside and out. God came in and declared war on satan and kicked satan and his demons out of my body, out of my life (even though they still showed themselves to me) so that I now could walk with Christ. Never ever doubt what God can do in your life. *Stand strong with God.*

"Continuing from *The Facts on the Occult* by John Ankerberg and John Weldon (pp 24–25). "Not surprisingly, there are many accounts of mediums, spiritists, and occultists—and these people who frequent them – suffering physically in a manner similar or identical to the symptoms described above. For example, the famous Russian medium, Ninel Kulagina, was the subject of repeated parapsychological experimentation. During some tests, her clothes would spontaneously catch on fire, and unusual burn marks would appear on her body. She "endured pain, long periods of dizziness, loss of weight, lasting discomfort," sharp spinal pain, blurred vision, and a near fatal heart attack from her psychic activities. Unfortunately, the heart attack was massive and left Kulagina a permanent invalid.

"The infamous "black" occultist, Aleister Crowley, ended up in an insane asylum for six months after trying to conjure the devil. His attempts to conjure helping spirits often produced demons instead. His children died, and his wives either went insane or drank themselves to death. Two biographers observed, "Every human affection that he had in his heart…was torn and trampled with such infernal ingenuity in his intensifying torture that his endurance is beyond belief." Crowley's tragedy illustrates an important point, that even with great knowledge and expertise in the occult, one is still not safe. And if experts in the occult aren't safe, how can anyone else guarantee their own protection?

Further, tragic "accidents" and other injuries also happen to the psychically involved and sometimes to their families. No less an authority than Dr. Koch has observed that people under occult subjection and demonization "frequently are in fatal accidents. I have many examples of this in my files." Elsewhere, he observes, "I would like to point out that in my own experience numerous cases of suicides, fatal accidents, strokes and insanity are to be observed among occult practitioners."

As we survey the world of the occult, it is easy to cite illustrations of such "accidents" and other consequences. The famous psychic surgeon, Arigo, died in a horrible car crash; the Russian occultist, Gurdjieff, nearly died in a fatal car accident. Well-known parapsychologist, Edmond Gurney, author of *Phantasms of the Living*, died a tragic death either by accident or suicide. "Christian" spiritualist William Branham died from a car accident; occult guru Rudrananda died at age 45 in a 1973 airplane crash.

The famous medium Eileen Garrett's parents both committed suicide; Krishnamurti's brother, Nityananda, died at age 25 and Krishnamurti himself experience terrible demonization throughout his life. He suffered incredibly strange and agonizing torments as part of a transforming "presence" he called "the process".

James I. Wedgwood, a Theosophy convert and leader of the Theosophically instituted Liberal Catholic Church, went mad for the last 20 years of his life-and we could mention scores of other illustrations. In our own studies, we have encountered heart attacks; epileptic seizures; mental derangement; strange blackouts; stomach; eye and skin problems; and many other maladies from occult practices.

During his lifetime, Dr. Koch counseled over 11,000 people who had encountered problems arising from their occult practices. He observes of those who carry on an active occult practice, "The family histories and the end of these occult workers are, in many cases known to me so tragic that we can no longer speak in terms of coincidence." For those *passively* involved, he observes that "occult subjection has been seen in relation to psychological disturbances, which have the following predominant characteristics:

a) Warping and distortion of character: hard, egotistical persons; uncongenial, dark natures.

b) Extreme passions: abnormal sexuality; violent temper, belligerence; tendencies to addiction; meanness and kleptomania.

c) Emotional disturbances: compulsive thoughts, melancholia; suicidal thoughts, anxiety states.

d) Possession: destructive urges, fits of mania; tendency to violent acts and crime....

e) Mental illnesses.

f) Bigoted attitude against Christ and God: conscious atheism; simulated piety; indifference to God's Word and prayer; blasphemous thoughts; religious delusions.

g) Puzzling phenomena in their environment.

Dr. Merrill F. Unger, author of four books on occultism and demonism, observes, "The psychic bondage and oppression that traffickers in occultism themselves suffer, as well as their dupes, is horrifying to contemplate."...

For two years, I went to the same church, and I would cry all through the sermons. I shed buckets of tears and used boxes of tissues. I would tell myself I was not going to cry anymore every time I went to church, but no matter how hard I tried to control my emotions, I couldn't stop myself from crying. The crying was God cleansing me from within, and a very necessary part of my growth as a Christian, and part of my healing. It wasn't all bad, though; people made friends with me and would invite me to go to lunch with them. I was still seeing Arthur and Angie but more as friends now. I was slowly beginning to trust other people little by little. I was running everything past God. I was changing my speech from New Age jargon to a more acceptable Christian language.

Ephesians 5:10-14 says, "Carefully determine what pleases the Lord. Take no part in the worthless deeds of evil and darkness; instead expose them. It is shameful even to talk about things that ungodly people do in secret. But their evil intentions will be exposed when the light shines on them, for the light makes everything visible. This is why it is said, "Awake, O sleeper, rise up from the dead, and Christ will give you light."

I still tried to carefully talk to the authorities in the church about the demonic stuff that I had seen there. But think about it, because of my past, they didn't really believe me. So, I said to them, "Please pray to the Holy Spirit, and He will tell you the truth." Just think, these people would have been Christians for many, many years, and who was I to say anything about what I had seen with my past? I had to give it over to God and leave it there. Again and again, this kind of thing happened to me.

Isn't it interesting I was never called a witch when I was on the dark side? In fact, I was treated with respect for what I knew. On God's side, it was a whole different story. God had spiritually and physically set me free, but do other Christians believe this? *No!* They had God, Jesus, and the Holy Spirit to pray to and ask if I was truly free. They would have had the Holy Spirit show them and have everything confirmed to them *if* they had *asked*. Ephesians 5:8-9 says, "For once you were full of darkness, but now you have light from the Lord. So live as people of light! For this light within you produces only what is good and right and true."

I was invited to my daughter's and her boyfriend's house for a party. My son was also going to be there. I felt that my daughter and son were putting me to the test because I knew that there was going to be drinking and drugs there. Did my son and daughter think that I would play holy and pure and not go? This was going to be my choice. I did ask people to pray for me, and they advised me not to go. I asked God, and He said, "Go," so I did. It was one of those dark and rainy nights. I decided to arrive around nine in the evening and planned to leave just before midnight. I drank ginger ale, as it looked like rye.

Darice's boyfriend had a good friend whom I instinctively knew was into witchcraft. He looked fine and completely normal, but he had many demons inside of him. I am going to call him Matthew. His girlfriend, whom I will call Tammy, seemed a really nice girl, and they had a relationship going on but lived in their own separate apartments. So, here we were at the party, lots of booze, good drugs, good night, but lots of ugly demons filled the house. I ended up talking to Matthew's girlfriend, Tammy. We connected right away. I told her about my life before the deliverance and how my life was taking shape now.

Matthew wanted to interrupt us. He was hovering around, listening to what we were talking about but trying to pretend that he wasn't. I could tell that he was not liking what was going on or what was being said. God said, "Look him directly in the eyes and don't back down. Be strong in me." I knew I was full of the Holy Spirit and stayed on course. Tammy knew that Matthew had deep spiritual problems. Ever since she had met him, she had experienced poltergeist activities in her apartment. She said that evil spirits were all over her apartment and that they would throw her about in her bedroom.

I knew she was telling me the truth. I told her that she was bound to Matthew and also that demons were having sex with her as well as with Matthew when they were having intercourse, and she was drowning from the inside out. Back at the party, as I looked around the room, I saw my son sitting in a chair, and there was this lime green slimy mist slowly moving around him. Then it spread out and moved on, gently touching others who were there. It was truly unholy! I asked the Lord, "Please let these people see what is around them. Let them see in the spiritual what I see and the demons that had crashed the party, then maybe they wouldn't do drugs and drink." God said, "*No*, my child." Why wouldn't God open their eyes to see all the evil there? Demons abound where drugs, alcohol, and sex are, as they feed off of what comes off of humans. God's heart must bleed for His people when He sees what we do and call it having a good time. My son told me later that he also saw this disgusting green slime. It totally freaked him out.

When I left the party that night, Matthew stayed out of my way. My God had me covered. Obviously, I needed to be there that night to talk to his girlfriend because she was really searching. After the party, she phoned a few times, and I took her out to lunch. I brought a prayer partner with me. I also asked Mike and a friend of his to pray for us whenever I went to see her. Then I went to her apartment and prayed. In the physical, her apartment wasn't dark, but in the spiritual, her place was extremely dark and gloomy. The heaviness of the place and the evil would make you depressed, and not surprisingly, she was depressed. I knew that Matthew was the source of this heaviness. She knew she should have left Matthew, and we discussed this, but she just couldn't let go. She phoned a couple more times, and then it was like she just disappeared. I prayed, "Dear God, keep her safe."

The last time I met with Tammy, she really didn't want to be with me, even though I treated her to lunch. She was determined to stay with Matthew. Spiritually, there was so little left of her; I knew this when I looked at her. She was being taken over completely it was horrible. I found out later that she and Matthew had split up and that she was very ill with Lyme disease and had to quit her job to get well. I felt very sad for her, but there was nothing I could do for her anymore. She had made her choice, and it had not been a good one.

CHAPTER 15

Change Over

One Sunday, I was put in the beginner's class in church. This was a class that taught you about the Bible, God, Jesus, and the Holy Spirit from a Christian perspective. It sets a foundation for your belief and faith. It was a good place for me. Later on in the church service, I was watching almost everybody raising their arms and praising Jesus. I thought (please forgive me, God), *You will not catch me doing that!* I thought they were pretending to be holy. The next morning on my day off, in my bedroom, Jesus spoke to me. They were words of life that penetrated into my soul and spirit. This next quote I received from Jesus is about true and false worship. Isaiah 58:1–14 says,

> "Shout with the voice of trumpet blast.
>   Shout aloud! Don't be timid.
> Tell my people Israel of their sins!
>   Yet they act so pious!
> They come to the Temple every day
>   and seem delighted to learn all about me.
> They act like a righteous nation
> that would never abandon the laws of its God.

They ask me to take action on their behalf,
pretending they want to be near me.
'We have fasted before you!' they say.
'Why aren't you impressed?
We have been very hard on ourselves,
and you don't even notice it!'

"I will tell you why!" I respond.
"It's because you are fasting to please yourselves.
Even while you fast,
you keep oppressing your workers.
What good is fasting
when you keep on fighting and quarreling?
This kind of fasting
will never get you anywhere with me.
You humble yourselves
by going through the motions of penance,
bowing your heads
like reeds bending in the wind.
You dress in burlap
and cover yourselves with ashes.
Is this what you are calling fasting?
Do you really think this will please the LORD?
"No, this is the kind of fasting I want:
Free those who are wrongly in prison;
lighten the burden of those who work for you.
Let the oppressed go free,
and remove the chains that bind people.
Share your food with the hungry,
and give shelter the homeless.
Give clothes to those who need them,
and do not hide from relatives who need your help.

"Then your salvation will come like the dawn,
and your wounds will quickly heal.
Your godliness will lead you forward,

and the glory of the LORD will protect you from behind.
Then when you call, the LORD will answer.
'Yes, I am here,' he will quickly reply.
"Remove the heavy yoke of oppression.
Stop pointing your finger and spreading vicious rumors!
Feed the hungry,
and help those in trouble.
Then your light will shine out from the darkness,
and the darkness around you will be as bright as noon.
The LORD will guide you continually,
giving you water when you are dry
and restoring your strength.
You will be like a well-watered garden,
like an ever-flowing spring.
Some of you will rebuild the desert ruins of your cities.
Then you will be known as a rebuilder of walls
and a restorer of homes.

"Keep the Sabbath day holy.
Don't pursue your own interest on that day,
but enjoy the Sabbath
and speak of it with delight as the LORD'S holy day.
Honor the Sabbath in everything you do on that day,
and don't follow your own desires or talk idly.
Then the LORD will be your delight
I will give you great honor
and satisfy you with the inheritance I promised to
your ancestor Jacob.
I, the LORD, have spoken!"

The parts of the above scripture that were illuminated for me
were verses 1 and then 8 through to 12.

What could Jesus do through me? I asked myself. Through my
tears, I was so touched by Jesus's presence. I asked forgiveness for the
day before when I was in church and I judged everyone who was lift-

ing arms and praising Jesus. I had said I would never do that. There was a big change in me in that area from that day on. I started to raise my hands in church and praise Jesus. I became part of the ministry team, for which Arthur and Angie were responsible. I didn't always take part, but I watched and prayed.

The enemy at first was very quick to try and trap me into believing that I was still theirs, and they could still effectively control me. One encounter I had with a demon changed all that. I was in a friend's apartment by myself when all of a sudden there was change in the atmosphere. It started to get colder. Then right in front of me, this blue/black demon showed up growing bigger very quickly. To me, he was at least nine feet tall and just as wide. There were billows of black smoke all around him. As for me, I was rooted to the spot. I was terrified! I couldn't move. Here came the fear that they were going to take me back. It then came right at me and enveloped me. I couldn't see anything as it totally surrounded me. Then I realized with great pleasure and relief that it had not gone through me. Here was the big change! Before my deliverance, it would have been able to pass through me. *Not* anymore! With my mind, I called out silently, "Jesus!" and the darkness was gone as fast as it had materialized. So, here was proof of the change within me. It was another big step forward.

I was still going to church learning about God, Jesus, and the Holy Spirit. I was still not fully accepting Jesus and the whole business with the cross. The enemy knew this, and one night when the store was closed, a group of demons came to visit me—uninvited, I might add—at the store. At this point in my walk, I was wearing a cross. This group of demons appeared at the bottom of the stairs leading up to my apartment. I would have to go through them to get up to my apartment. I had to learn something here. I pulled the cross out and held it up in front of them, expecting them to vanish as quickly as they had appeared. *No!* They just laughed at me and said, "You still don't believe in the cross." And so they stayed. I was stunned. I just stood there, it was true. I still didn't understand the cross. What an eye-opener. Now I knew, but I knew they couldn't touch me, nor were they trying to. They just stayed right where they had appeared. I cried out, "Help me, Father, Jesus, and the Holy Spirit!" and walked towards them, praising the Lord, and the demons vanished immediately. Lesson learned: don't kid yourself about how strong you think you are in the Lord. You by yourself are not invincible. The demons have studied all of us for far too long! There was a deficiency in my armor. I had to get with the program and learn more about the cross which I did.

Coming across from darkness into the light, I foolishly thought that being delivered would make my life somehow easier with images of lovely thatched cottages, roses around the doors, contentment, and peace. This life was a struggle, requiring a lot of effort and determination to stay on the right track and much more. Looking on the bright side of things, the Lord had His hand on my life. The right people were coming into my life at the right times so I could keep moving on and growing. I still wonder how God got me through all that He got me through so that I can stand where I am today. This is God's miracle in my small life. Miraculously, He pulled me through. I look back, and I just don't know how He did it, but He did it! For He is the great I AM!.

With what I had been into, there was an enormous amount of problems that needed Christ's healing touch. Enlighten me, Lord, please, for it seems that as fast as I am growing and feeling cleaner from the inside out, my flesh and body were extremely uncomfortable with the same. I was feeling dirty. There was a physical and spiritual discomfort within myself, and then God gave me a dream. When I was a child, we had this family dog. He went everywhere we went and was a great bodyguard. Every week my mother would make sure he had a bath. No dirty dogs in her house. The dog hated the baths; as soon as he could, he would sneak away to the local sewage plant and roll in whatever he thought smelt nice and then come home smelling disgusting and smiling.

God showed me that this was what I was doing. Having been spiritually unclean for so long, my physical body did not feel comfortable with God's cleanup of my life. To overcome what was going on, I was to relax with it and let God be God in my life. I confess that I didn't understand all the pros and cons of this. Acts 10:14-15 says, "No, Lord," Peter declared. "I have never eaten anything that our Jewish laws have declared impure and unclean." But the voice (God) spoke again. "Do not call something unclean if God has made it clean."

There have been a few people in my past who have deemed me "unclean," people that probably should have known better. All I need to concern myself with is that my God tells me "I am clean."

CHAPTER 16

Peanut in the Desert

I was talked into going to a Christian retreat up north. It was a three-day, two-night event. You had to leave your car on shore and boat across to the lodge. I didn't like this idea at all. For the weekend, it was log cabins, insects, etc. I shared a room with a friend, but I was definitely out of my comfort zone. I wasn't comfortable with having so many people that I did not know around me. I tried to keep a smile on my face. If I could have walked on water back to my car after the first day there, I would have left with not even a good-bye note. Friday evening, everybody was in the main room at the lodge. The Holy Spirit's presence was so strong I could not enter that room. So, I pulled a chair up to the door and just sat there and cried and cried. One of the ladies ministered to me, and then I went to bed.

Saturday night was totally different. The whole Christian group was praising God and dancing, bunny-hopping, jumping up and down in one spot. It looked weird to me, so I just watched. On the other side, I was taught to dance for the "angels of light," and I didn't want to dance anymore. All of a sudden, the room changed, and Jesus stood in front of me and said, "Dance for me, child." "No," I said. "I can't." That is what I did before for the spirits, and it was wrong. Jesus said, "Do this for me." I felt I was released, and I danced for Him and only Him. It was wonderful to worship Jesus that way. When I stopped dancing, I didn't realize that everybody in the group had stopped to watch me, not that it had mattered. The important part was that I had been set free from yet another part of my previous life, just as it was with the semiprecious stones.

Sunday was the last day of the retreat, and I wanted nothing to do with the "spiritual" anymore; fifty years of my life was enough. To me, it was too dangerous, and I didn't want any repeats of my past. I also wanted to know that I was really clean. I knew the tricks the enemy could play, how they twisted things, and how easy it was to be deceived. I did not want to be slain in the spirit. Let me explain— being slain in the spirit is a process where someone who is full of the Holy Spirit prays for you right beside you, and the presence of the Lord can become so strong you fall down, similar to fainting but not quite the same. Even though you fall down and can't get up for a while, you are aware of what is going on around you. I was still not very trusting and suspicious of anything spiritual. This freaked me out because I had a fear of going down; it was like being hypnotized to me, and I would not be in control. I also didn't want anything entering me again after my experiences with the evil spirits. I was determined to not be slain in the spirit. I figured it was safer this way.

Arthur prayed for me, and the Holy Spirit spoke to me and was very gentle. Then almost against my will, down I went. In my mind, I was saying to myself, *I am not going to go down*. But down I went, anyway. Then the Holy Spirit whispered in my ear as I lay on the floor, "Watch me, child," He said. He took this beautiful double-edged sword so bright it looked amazing, and then He passed it through my whole body from my head to my feet. Then He said to me, "Do you think anything evil could have stayed there with what I just did with the sword? You are clean, my child." I believe in what was said, yet another milestone was overcome.

God showed me that I had never really ever been a child, teenager, or young adult. My past had always been clouded over by the spirits within me. He was now giving me grace to catch up with all the things I had missed as part of growing up. Not bonding with my children was another important thing I had never yet experienced. I remember being so shocked when I read about how important it is to bond with your children. Then Jesus showed me a picture of my soul. It was so scarred and damaged there were holes in it. It was bleeding and septic. He then showed me the same picture again two years later, and there was no comparison. My soul now looked alive and fresh. Psalm 23:1–3 says, "The Lord is my shepherd, I shall not be in want. He makes me lie down in green pastures, he leads me beside quiet waters, he restores my soul."

Another problem I had early on in my walk with God was He told me I could no longer leave my body. This is known as an out-of-body experience. As a child, my father would be hitting me, and I would escape by leaving my body, and then I would return when the punishment was over. Leaving my body was as easy as breathing. I found it harder to do when he would sit me in a chair and play cat and mouse games (as I would call it) with me, never knowing when I would get hit. I guess when this happened, it would arouse fear so strong that I had a hard time leaving my body with the usual ease. I was distressed when God said I had to stop. God calmed me down and touched me, so I forgot about this incident and dilemma until about eighteen months later. Then God touched me again and said, "See, staying in your body was not so bad after all." I had totally forgotten how I used to leave my body until God reminded me. I realized in that moment how comfortable I now was in my own body since I had become a Christian and really believed in God. You have got to love God's finishing school; He does not miss a trick. He was undoing all the things the enemy of my soul had taught me to do.

Praising and worshiping the Lord was still another big problem for me. I didn't like it. The Holy Spirit said this is needed in your life as a child of God. At first, I bought Christian CDs and praise and worship tapes that had no singing on them, just instrumental music that was Christian-based. I played them twenty-four hours a day in the store and my apartment. I kept on playing them in my car and bedroom so I could sleep, as sleeping was still a problem for me. I have since learned that David used to play praise and worship music to King Saul to bring peace to his troubled soul after the Lord had put a tormenting spirit within him (1 Samuel 16:14–23).

I then eventually progressed to worshiping, to music, and then later the words, but it seemed such a slow process. Then every night after ten in the evening, when the store was closed and I was by myself, I would go to the back of the store and play praise music to my Lord, even lifting my hands up to Him, pouring out my broken heart. He established a relationship with me using worship. I didn't realize how very important this was in my walk with Him. There is only one way to say it—God bonded with me. Unbelievable to me, but it's true. This has held me in good stead in the last twenty-five years of my walk with my God. My relationship was with God first and then the church, not the other way round. God would say to me, first you minister to me and then others as I direct you.

Two years into my Christian walk, I still felt that the process was so slow. Things seemed to be going okay, and then suddenly— *bang*!—everything would go upside down again. I had seen over and over again what the spirits could do to people, and again I became afraid that they would be able to take me back, and I would be in their clutches once more. On the other hand, God my Father was always kind, compassionate, and very caring. I went before Him and said, "I need to see your power. Show me your power and authority. I have only seen satan's." He lifted me up, and I had a bird's-eye view of a desert—billions of grains of sand. To me, it seemed like the Sahara Desert. As far as my eye could see, there was sand and more sand. God said, "This represents how vast my power is." Okay, I said, I then started looking for satan's power. "Where is he?" I asked, as I couldn't see him (satan). Then my Heavenly Father said, "Do you see that little peanut down in the right-hand corner of the desert?" "Yes," was my reply. "Good, now watch, little one. One small puff of wind and I have him completely covered by sand." How vast is our God and how small is satan in comparison.

Another shock was coming my way. The demons that had controlled me had made it very easy for me to buy the store because it was in their territory. With my second husband, I had the store for thirteen years before I was delivered. It was strange; I lost a large percentage of my native customers when I changed from the darkness to God's light. By the time I had sold the store, I had had it for twenty-two years. I still had money put away; I was not rich, but I was doing okay.

Now the Lord started asking me if I loved Him. That was easy, I answered, "Yes, Lord, I love you." Then some time later, He asked, "Gloria, do you love me?" "Of course, I love you, Lord. Why do you keep on asking?" Then He asked me the third time, and all the red lights should have gone on. I said, "Yes, Lord, yes, I love you." Then here came the shock. Every one of my machines in the store broke down, and I had a lot of machines—one after the other. Things had to be fixed, replaced, and goodness knows what else. All of the money that I had put away was gone towards new or repaired equipment and machinery, and I cried, "I needed that money as my backup! Why did this happen, Lord?" The answer came back from the Lord loud and very clear. "You are making money your security blanket. I am your security blanket. The money you saved was dirty money given to you by the demons, and this has no place in your life now." I was shocked and had no control over these incidents whatsoever. Who says God doesn't do this kind of thing? Well, I want to tell you, He does. God was showing me that I was putting money before Him.

Money had been my security blanket for a very long time. But now it was gone, and I had to now readjust my walk with my Savior. No way did I want to go back to my "old life." My path was with God. I forgot to mention that there was about $400 left of my backup money. God nudged me and persuaded me to give that money to a missionary trip that was going to Haiti. Here was reverse psychology. Enemy money was being used against them, the demons, in a dominion that they ruled over Haiti. I liked God's plan. All of that unclean money had to go, and it did. Did I do that? No! God did it. Another lesson learned.

CHAPTER 17

A Fire at Halloween: Trick or Treat

T ongue in cheek as I say this, I was something of a novelty at the church. Looking back, God put me in the right church with the right people for where I was at at the time. They mentioned more than once how open, truthful, and transparent I was about everything. I thought, should you not be more truthful than me, as you are the religious people, not me? They would preach Jesus to me, but it was easy for me to see that not all of them really believed in Christ. I said this to some of them, and alas, it didn't go down very well. I was also told that people at the church were learning through my testimony that the devil is real. I must say that I was totally disgusted, mortified, and embarrassed that demons could be walking around inside a church. The demons would look at me, making sure I knew that they had the right to be there. So many people in the church were like puppets, dressed alike, spoke alike, and went to the same places alike, masquerading, pretending. God did not create puppets; He created masterpieces, individuals with Jesus at the head.

Some well-meaning ladies at the church felt they should tell me I would be kept for a long time at the bottom of the pecking order at this church. They said to me, "Don't expect gifts from God because of your background." They told me that I was prideful and that I should know my place and that it would be a long time before God would give me words to share with other people. I think they were trying to tell me that I was still unclean and that I would have to prove myself. (My thoughts on this were just like Cinderella and the three ugly sisters—funny, what? Just my sense of humor.) This upset me, and I cried, but I got over it.

As I left the church and walked towards my car, the same ladies were standing by one of the ladies' vehicles all together. I walked over to them and told them to never ever talk to me that way again. I said to them, "How dare you. Do you think you are God's personal assistants?" I told them in no uncertain terms that I was so glad I wasn't a wimpy, vulnerable new believer, as they could have so easily crushed my spirit. I was so angry with them I told them they were not doing the work of God but helping satan out immensely. Were they in the right place with God? I then left them and walked to my car. I put this down to another learning curve. My conclusion later was that some Christians eat their own. It reminded me of a praying mantis that eats her mate alive.

I once read about a lady who came to her local church and in time became a Christian. As days went by, she became more involved with that church family. I don't know the details, but she had a history of sin that was well known in the community. One day, the church met together, and someone raised the question of this woman's past reputation. Some expressed concern about her past and how her presence and example might reflect on the church in the local community. A lively discussion took place about her. Her character was being challenged, as in the past, she had been a prostitute, but that was about fifteen years prior to giving her life to Christ through God.

Finally, someone wisely stood up and made their point. The person said, "What is on trial here in this discussion is not this woman and her past. What is on trial here is the blood of Jesus Christ. Is it sufficient to cleanse her? When we face a sense of condemnation, self-accusations, and feeling like we are on trial before God and our own conscience, remember it's not you but the blood of Jesus that is on trial." Was Jesus's death sufficient for me? Not only he died for us, but we are regarded as having died in Christ. His death is our death, and on that basis, we have been justified fully and freely. It is done. We are free from our sins and are clean.

God had taken away all of my spiritual gifts on the dark side, and over a period of time, He cleaned me up and gave them back to me one by one. So many things that the people in church said, that I would never have such gifts ever again, but I was slowly realizing that I would have them again. God gave them back to me to be used for His glory forever and ever. At the same time, I was asked to officially join the church I was attending and was invited to be a "member." I thought that it was a good sign that I was being accepted by my fellow Christian friends; after all, God had told me that I needed to be attending a church. I felt I had maybe made the grade, but I had the wrong idea entirely. Such things I know now are from the ego. Even though I felt honored to be accepted as a member of the church, something was not right about it. So, I took this before my Father (God) in prayer. The answer came back, "No, child, you will get too involved with the church. You will be busy with church things and forget about me." My father is very wise; He was correct.

Slowly, the Lord started giving me words and directions for people. I have to tell you that I was very careful and nervous and would take it all before Him again in prayer. And then the Lord would confirm it. There is one example of a message I had for one particular lady early in my Christian walk. She went to a different church than myself. She had a lovely home with a swimming pool. With some friends, we were invited over for a baptism in her pool with a barbecue after. God kept putting her right in front of me. Why? He had a word for her. She was dabbling with New Age, and it would be better if she stopped, as she had no idea what she was getting into. I was told to warn her. God always told me that He would take me back into what He had taken me out of, which was the occult (and that is an abomination to Him). God did this so that I could talk freely into people's lives about the bondages I had been under and warn them so they can make better choices in their lives. I didn't know this woman. I struggled mightily to have the courage to give her this word from

God, but because I was resisting what God wanted me to do, I felt as if my insides were melting. Was I being disobedient? Yes!

In the end, I gave in and gave the words to her from God. But I am sad to say that it was more with embarrassment than anything else that I delivered God's message to her. The lady understood exactly what I was talking about and said that she would deal with it. My sheepish behavior did not put me in good standing with the Lord. He didn't shout or raise His voice at me, but He told me to never be embarrassed about Him again. After that, I was sobbing down on the floor in my home, arms stretched out, begging Him to forgive me. He did; His grace is so amazing. I was in the wrong, and I knew it. That lady needed the word given to her, and she knew it. Don't ever be embarrassed for giving a word to someone that was given to you from our mighty God. Here was another lesson learned.

It is worth mentioning an important aspect of being a Christian at this point. Some people when they are given a word don't check it out with the Holy Spirit first. They just decide that they don't like it, so either they try to kill the messenger or they forget it and put in a bin. You would be shocked how many times this happens, total rejection of our God's living Word. I asked God, why didn't He just come out and tell me before I went to that lady's house, as it would have been easier to tell me right up front? I probably would have done a much better job of giving her the message. Right away back came His answer, "Because, my child, maybe number one, you would just not have given her the message at all, or maybe number two, you would have become puffed up with pride." It was true in both cases. I am so glad that my God loves and knows me, for He created me.

It was also at this same time that the babies and the young ones that were in the church nursery were not happy. The nursery was where the children slept and played, but the atmosphere was very heavy and not good. People had prayed over the nursery, but still the spiritual atmosphere was not healthy in the nursery rooms. One Saturday morning, the whole church was called in to pray around the church and the property. I was asked if I would like to join in. We prayed in the church first. Then we all went outside, and people split up into groups, praying (and just chatting) as they walked around the building and the grounds. I hung back so I could be by myself. I walked around the building slowly. There was a grassy part near the front door of the church. In the ground, I saw this huge slug-like creature. It had a round face, which it lifted up towards me. It had no problem telling me that it had been living in the grounds around the church for years, and it went in and out of the nursery at will. It went where it wanted to go. Its lair was underground in a marshy place to the left of the church.

I told the creature that resembled a huge slug that it had no right to be there because it was hallowed ground. The creature just laughed at me. "I have every right to be here," it replied. There was no fear in this creature. The groups of people had sprinkled holy oil on various parts of the grounds, praying as they went. The creature still had no problem moving over holy oil, and there was no way it was planning on moving out of its territory. As people came around the building to where I was standing, the slug vanished. My first thought was to tell Arthur what was going on. The Lord said, "*No, Arthur would not believe you, but report it to the deacon.*" Two or three days later, I went to see the man, and I told him what I had seen and what the creature had said. Looking at his face, I think he thought I was hallucinating. God was with me so strongly, and I pressed in. "Now that you have this information," I said, "you can pray better for what is coming against the church." He just told me to leave it with him. I really don't know all the details of what he did or said to the authorities in the church. I do know that there was a praise, prayer, and fasting night at the church, and as far as I knew, everything was cleansed, and lots of changes came about. I still had questions, though, about this evil slug. I knew that for it to live in the ground, the earth must have been unhallowed. The church had been built right over its hunting ground. I wondered what had happened there centuries ago. Furthermore, why didn't the holy oil burn its body? The land God has given us is very dear to His heart. But do we keep the land the Lord has given us spiritually clean? Sometimes people need to know what they are praying against and ask the Holy Spirit to show them how they should be praying. If we are in right standing with our God, He will place the right prayer in our hearts.

The Holy Spirit will give us the words to use to pray. Sometimes we need to keep praying consistently until the Holy Spirit tells us it is done.

Less than six months after my deliverance, along comes Halloween. I used to love Halloween. The store would be decorated, and the staff would dress up. There was coffee and cookies for the parents and goodies for all the children, and I would get between three or four hundred children coming to the store on Halloween night. The kids told me that they had spent their money in my store all year, and so this was payback time. I always made sure I had good stuff to give them. This year, after my deliverance, it was going to be different—it had to be. Before I was a Christian, I used to order from the gift shows held in Toronto masks, makeup, costumes, and all the things that went along with Halloween. This year, I was very careful with what masks I picked for the store, even the candy I was giving out. Everything had to be changed, and I was changed as well. I decided it would be better if I didn't work that night. Two of my staff dressed up as clowns. I went to a friend's house and came back after the store was closed and before the big kids came out to play (the over-eighteen-year-olds). This was a village tradition.

I went up to the apartment around ten thirty in the evening, put on a movie, and started to watch *Robin Hood* (Kevin Costner was Robin Hood). An American actor playing an English part doesn't work. There was a witch in the movie, so I turned it off and went to bed. The next thing I hear is men banging on the store door downstairs, yelling, "Are you up there? The store is on fire!" I thought, *Good trick, guys.* It is Halloween, past midnight, and since I couldn't smell smoke, I checked out the windows. I didn't see anything, so I got back into bed. The yelling continued, and I recognized some of the voices. They were going to break down the store door because what I didn't realize and couldn't see was that the flames were leaping above my forty-foot building. I grabbed my purse, housecoat, and downstairs I went. There really was a fire! Somebody had started it at the back of the building. Flames were shooting upwards, well over the top of the roof. The insulation in the store walls was dry crushed cork. The place should have gone up like a tinderbox with me in it. Where the fire had been started, I would have been trapped.

The volunteer fire brigade had been called to another fire, and they had just rounded the corner and saw what was happening to my building. So, they stopped and were able to put the fire out before going onto their next call. All the siding on the back side of the store had melted. The fire didn't go inward; instead it shot up into the sky. Only the outside of the store was damaged. The electrical wires on the inside of the back walls had not even melted. The insurance adjuster, when checking the damages, said, "Lady, somebody upstairs must have been looking after you. With what you have for insulation in the walls and with how old and dry this building is, this place should not be here now." It was God looking after me again. Nobody could believe how little damage the fire actually did, but I believe because God was in my life; however, I was still very upset with the whole thing. Obviously, revenge was what the demons wanted and me burned. God had other ideas. I am so glad I never found out who had started that fire; otherwise, I would have gone after them. I was so consumed by anger that I would have used my shotgun and gone after whoever had done it and worried about the consequences later. My thoughts at the time were that this was a conspiracy between man and the demons that wanted to get even with me. Why?

It took a while after that for me to settle down. What I saw a week later was that the flames went up and not inwards. That was God! I wasn't harmed in any way. That was God. It was business as usual the next day in the store. In fact, the store was *really* busy when everyone had heard what had happened. The only problem was me. Why did all this weird stuff happen to me? Writing this and looking back, I was still growing in the understanding of God's love for me. No matter what the demons were trying to do, God kept making what they did null and void. I was still struggling with trust and wanting to strike back because I was dealing with rejection, fear, hurt, and feeling alone. Then the Lord one night gave me a wonderful word from the Bible: "No one will be able to stand up against you all the days of your life. As I was with Moses, so I will be with you;

I will never leave you nor forsake you. Be strong and courageous" (Joshua 1:5–6).

I was told that you can have *nothing* in your possession that you hold dear from the other side. You can be delivered, but by holding onto these items, this gives the demons a right to come back into your life. Who spiritually has your body? Take into account that there is *no* middle road here, so do you belong to God or satan? If it isn't God, please try reading my testimony again.

If you really think Halloween is fun, you should be asking God and checking it out because really it is very deadly and should be avoided if you say you are a Christian. Halloween celebrates witchcraft. By celebrating it, you are adding to their power and honoring satan. But who am I to tell you this? I had to find this out for myself the hard way.

If you have been following my somewhat turbulent and nerve racking life so far, I hope the next pieces of information gleaned from the Bible will be of some interest to you.

In the Old Testament demons are only mentioned twice. Deuteronomy 32:17; and Psalm 106:37.

From various biblical passages in the Old Testament it shows evil spirits/demons working behind the occult, spiritualism and the supernatural. In Deuteronomy 18:9-12; I Samuel 28;7-13; and Isaiah 8:19; God denounces *all* such practices.

It struck me interesting that people would consult magicians, sorcerers, astrologists, mediums, witches and psychics, but not our God, who created us. And this is happening extensively in our world today. Who do you consult?

The New Testament has no problem mentioning satan and demons. Just like us they have the capacity to speak, hear, think, feel and act as *we* do. Quite able to take orders and diligently carry them out. Matthew 8:31; 17:18; Mark 1:34, 5:12; Luke8:32, 10:17.

Demons hate us and can oppress us, causing mental disorders and sickness. Matthew 4:24; 12:22; 15:22; Luke 4:35 and madness, Mark 5:2-20; Luke 8:27-29.

Remember I *was* demon-possessed. Jesus whenever He saw people with this affliction would drive the demons out and deliver the persons from their sufferings and torture at their hands. Jesus exorcizes demons. Matthew 8:28-34; Mark 5:1-20; Luke 8:26-39; Matthew 12:22-32; Mark 3:22-27; Luke 11:14-23. Hallelujah!

The Book of Acts describes exorcisms, read Acts 19:13-20. One thing I have learnt, No demons or persons can control or duplicate God's awesome power.

If you are mixed up in the occult, black magic, or sorcery, learn a lesson from the Ephesians and get rid of anything that can trap you in such practices.

There was talk at the church among the singles group that I had become part of that I should take a group of them to the store so I could show them my life there. They were inquisitive and curious about me. I was skeptical because I said to the Lord they would come out and judge me as I sold lottery tickets (gambling), cigarettes, which is smoking, and rented movies that were of the world (not Christian). I didn't want to do this, so I prayed to the Lord about this and got His confirmation to invite the singles group to my home and store. It would be an eye-opener for them, I thought. The visit went well. Though I could see that some of them seemed shocked at what they saw, they never said anything about it.

Over time, I removed the things that didn't serve the Lord from my store. This was by the leading of the Holy Spirit. Everything has to happen in the Lord's time and at His command. Bit by bit, my life was changing for the better. My transformation was not going to happen overnight.

The church was arranging to take a dinner cruise. I was invited to come along. Thinking it would be good for me, I said yes. As part of the cruise, we would be visiting the Six Nations native reserve. We would all meet at the church and then take a coach to where the boat was waiting for us. This would mean a whole day on a boat, seeing the sunset, and weather permitting. I was thinking that I would be safe among Christians was looking forward to it. There were about forty in total going on the cruise. It was a chance for me to get to know people better as well.

I was still reserved around people and felt more comfortable being alone. I was still not very trusting of other people. The coach ride to where the boat was moored was fun. As we got there, the weather became bright and sunny. As we boarded the boat, I saw the six young people who would be serving us for dinner. Immediately, I felt the darkness around them. Then I saw that most of them were wearing crystals around their necks and dressed in black, which could have been their uniform, and the girls were wearing dark makeup, black nail polish, and black lipstick. Ugh!

I am asking myself a question, what was wrong? I was in a boat with forty Christians plus a couple of pastors and their wives. This was offset by the six young people who were going to be serving us, and I knew they were into the New Age crap. Why didn't the other people on the boat sense what I sensed? Stop! I wanted to cry out. I thought this to myself, *Please let us pray to God so that we are not prey to the enemy.* I just about had a panic attack, so I disappeared into the washroom and vomited. I felt better, but I was screaming out in my thoughts, *God, where are you?*

Things got worse. I couldn't eat what they served, and I now had a splitting headache. I was doing the human thing and trying to look like I was having a good time. After dinner, I went to the back of the boat and stayed out of the way. Next, the boat stopped at one of the native islands. The native people were selling their goods, and again I stayed back. To me, certain items were very spiritual, and from where I had come from then, it would be wise for me to stay clear of them. An example of what I saw there are dream catchers. To me they were creepy. At long last, we were back on the coach going home. The girl who had sat next to me on the way had changed places with another woman who wanted to talk to me. Well, this young lady had demons. I wanted to say to her, "Could you please sit somewhere else because I didn't want to be harassed by what was inside of you?" But instead, I sat there, being harassed by them all the way back into London. My headache was getting worse. I had double vision, I felt sick, and the atmosphere around her and me was very thick. I felt I was under a brutal attack. How tense can it get, and who would believe me? The entire event was a disaster to me, and no one else seemed to be aware of all the evil around them. I was ultra-sensitive to spirits after coming out of what I had just come out of, so everyone else had a really good day except yours truly. My headache got worse and worse. Now I am off the bus and back into my car. It is very late. I still had to drive back to Melbourne. I was sick on the way home and still had double vision and was anxious and not coping well. "I am under attack, help me, Lord," I prayed.

I spent the next day in bed, too sick to do anything. How do you rate that? It wasn't the people's fault, so what happened? That day had been very difficult for me. Lord God, help me make it. The one thing I didn't want to do was go back to church because all the same people would be there that were on the boat trip. I was thinking that I would be safe, being around Christians, but nothing could be further from the truth. I labeled the church as I labeled myself, it was like Waterloo Station at rush hour for demons and unclean spirits, just like I had been. What happens to people like myself who are delivered but still very vulnerable to things that most people cannot see? And these things, unclean spirits and demons, still think that those of us who are saved are still theirs, and they demand that we go back to them. No way! No way am I ever going back! This event did make me realize how weak I was, but God never left me. I had missed God's point! God was showing me to put faith in Him, not other Christians. They were not my protection; *God* was. As much as I had been into the wrong spiritual realms, it was as if I now had to go even deeper the other way. From the depths to the utmost, only God could get me there. My faith was weak, but I was surely growing but not fast enough for my liking.

Yet another incident happened with me being a Christian. There were problems at the church I was going to. A young married man with children was trying to seduce young babysitters either at his house or when he was taking them home. The church authorities were trying to keep it hush-hush, but it was leaking out all over the place. His parents were in very good standing with the church, but he was obviously having some lust problems. One of his victims was the daughter of a pastor and his wife who had been teaching me at the new beginners class in the church. One day, the pastor's wife phoned me and said she would like to talk to me about all that was happening to her daughter. So, I went and talked to her, and five hours later, I was on my way home. The talk had gone well, and God was there with us.

It was late, about one in the morning, and there was a dark stretch of road. I began to feel cold (as soon as I start to feel cold when I am warm, I always know that something is about to happen), and while I was looking ahead, I could see two sets of headlights coming towards me quite fast from on the other side of the road. Then suddenly, the lights started bobbing around all over the road, and they came over to my side. A voice loud and clear said, "Pray, Gloria, pray!" The lights were coming at me so fast that even though I had taken my foot off the accelerator, they were upon me. God kept my hands steady on the wheel. Two of the large lights went over top of the car. The other two went to each side of the car. I was sweating and still praying. I put my foot down on the gas and headed for home as fast as I could. I thanked the Lord for saving me because if I had gone off the road there, the car would have surely rolled. I was shaken up but safe. God had been with me.

I was asked why I didn't look in my mirror to see what was going on. I thought, give me a break, what was coming at me was not of God. God told me to pray, and I did. Better the Lord look after it, for He is all-knowing. I wondered what the Christian who asked me this would have done if it had happened to him. Am I lying? Am I making these stories up? Am I perhaps on drugs or just having a vivid imagination? Unless you have walked in my shoes and had my life, don't try to figure it out and do not judge me. God made me, and He knows me. Nothing else matters. Whatever the enemy was trying to do, God had me covered. It just wasn't always comfortable, calm, or tranquil.

CHAPTER 18

God Performs a Deliverance

One Christmas, after Fred had left me, Darice, her boyfriend, Greg, and I were together. They all bought me a complete new outfit for Christmas. Then they had an added surprise. Darice and I had two front row seats for the show *Phantom of the Opera*. What a night. Watching how the Phantom (the devil) controlled that girl was like my life passing in front of my eyes. I shed a lot of tears throughout that performance, and they were good tears. God was showing me that He had set me free. I bought a black and white picture of the phantom mask with a white rose. I just had to buy it. The next day, God spoke to my heart and said, "Gloria, I am the rose, and by my grace, you were set free and are free indeed. I as the rose stand between you and the enemy of your soul." So many times (please forgive me, Lord) I have been so scared that the enemy would get me back and I would be lost forever. But that was not God's plan for my life. Dear God and Jesus, I declare myself totally dependent upon you. I want to be everything you created me to be in you, and I want *it all!*

Reflecting back on my life again, so many times I wanted to escape from it, to block out so many memories. Mentally, I am not sure what I did with all these "stories." I pushed them down within me into a steel box, put a steel lid on the top, and locked it in all four corners. God was working on that tight lid, gradually unlocking and letting stuff out piece by piece and dealing with every piece. Even as I am writing this book, this healing is still happening. Amazing grace, O God, give me the courage to face my past and move on into your light today in Jesus's name. Darice, my daughter, lived with me at the store for about two years while she was going to university. We were getting along fine. She had left a long-term relationship, and I told her she could come and live with me for as long as she needed to.

One night, something rather strange started to happen with her. I kept looking at her, thinking something had changed and not for the better. But when I looked at her, nothing was there. I thought it was my imagination, and I would let it go. "I really do love my daughter." I had decided to give her a farewell party before she left to go work up north for the summer. I invited some friends around the night before she was going to leave. All the guests arrived, and everybody was having a good time. It was organized on a night the store closed early. I kept sensing that Darice was watching me, but when I looked at her, she wasn't looking at me. It was strange. Around midnight, all the guests had left, and we were cleaning up. Darice was at the sink washing dishes, and I was putting stuff away. Then she lost her temper with me. She told me I had interrupted her when she was talking to some of her friends and that I had butted in between herself and another person, etc.

There were other things that she was angry at me for. I was looking at her, thinking, *Darice, where are you coming from?* I thought that with her going up north, maybe we needed to have this out now before she goes. *Okay*, I thought, *I am going to tell her what I think.* I was counting to ten, and then I was going to explode on her, but at four, the Lord spoke to me and said, "We are going to have a deliverance here tonight." I thought that that was a little strange because I had already told God that I didn't want to deal with any deliverances or spiritual stuff ever again. He just said, "The Bible is on your desk, start reading the Psalms." All this time, Darice was still going on about things I had done to upset her. At this point, I wasn't really listening to her but listening to God.

Here she is still at the sink, and there I am at the desk, reading the Psalms quietly. As I did this, the presence of the Lord came into the room more and more. Darice was now standing by the side of the counter when the Lord said, "Watch, Gloria." As I looked, I could see this thing (demon) that was within Darice, wriggling. I watched fascinated, still trying to read Psalms. The more the Lord's presence came into the room, the harder the thing in Darice tried to stay inside of her, but it couldn't. It slowly came up within her body and eventually came out through the top of her head and vanished. I knew she had been delivered of something. We hugged, and the Lord's love was so strong in the room; anything evil could not have stayed.

At about two in the morning, we went to bed and had to get up at five in order for her to catch the Greyhound bus to go north. We slept really well. We talked on the way into the station. Darice's personality had changed, and she was back to being the Darice I knew. We hugged each other and said our good-byes, and then I came back home. I was astonished and amazed. I had not asked God to deliver her of anything. Why didn't I see she had something inside her? I had not even laid hands on her (although I wanted to but not in that way). I just had to watch, and God did the deliverance, although He did say, "We are going to have a deliverance here tonight." I thanked God for what He did. To this day, she doesn't remember what happened that evening after the guests had left.

For the last four years, I had been living at the store on my own. It was very difficult for me. I was having growing pains as I grew slowly into a Christian and was releasing daily the fears from my previous life. I often felt caught in the middle, not sure whether to step forward or back. So often I was anxious and fearful, but whenever I was most unsure about things, I would focus and pray to my God, and He always saw me through. Bit by bit, I was being transformed into the new me. All through my transformation to being Christian, I was reading the Bible more and more, as it helped remind me that even though I was now on the right side of the spiritual journey, it still was not always easy, far from it. I refer you to this particular scripture as it gave me strength and made me realize that I was not the only one having these problems during my Christian walk.

"We are pressed on every side by troubles, but we are not crushed. We are perplexed, but not driven to despair. We are hunted down, but never abandoned by God. We get knocked down, but we are not destroyed" (2 Corinthians 4:8-9).

PART 3

Early Days as a Christian

CHAPTER 19

Priorities in the Right Order!

Life went on for me in the same old daily routine. Back we go again. God was keeping me very sheltered not only in the store but during my time off. I didn't realize it, but I needed all the protection I could get. The Holy Spirit kept touching me. I had a sense that He was with me, and I could always sense His presence. The reason for touching me was that the apartment upstairs needed a makeover. The Holy Spirit was guiding me to make a change. I had been living there for thirteen years on the wrong side of the track. I now wanted out of the whole existence, the store, living above the store and basically anything to do with the store. If there was to be a makeover in my apartment, it meant to me that God would be keeping me there. Why would the apartment get a makeover when I wanted out? "No way," I said. "No makeover!" The weeks went by, but the Holy Spirit still made me aware that a makeover was necessary. One Monday morning, on my day off, He was *so* persistent. I yelled out at Him and said, "Okay, I will go and look at furniture." I remember being very annoyed and impatient with Him. Didn't God get it? I didn't want to stay there. I wanted to sell the place so I could get on with *my life* (not my life in God).

With a friend, I went into London, Ontario, just to look. Ha! By the end of the day, I had bought all new living room furniture, new bedroom furniture, carpets, lamps, and whatever else I needed. It was a God day, only I didn't realize it. Driving home as I came back from the furniture store, it was late and dark. I had just crossed over the Melbourne borderline and was just coming into the village when there was this tremendous flash of light that stayed all around me inside and outside the car. I did not know how I didn't go off the road. Then my God's voice spoke through the light. "Gloria, the lighthouse is in place." (I knew immediately it was the store.) "But I (God) am having a little problem with the lighthouse keeper." The lighthouse keeper was me, of course.

I am still driving. I see the store, but it has now become this gigantic lighthouse throwing rays of light out all over the countryside. I pulled up in the parking lot, and everything was back to normal except for me. I cried and cried and said, "Please forgive me, Lord." I was at the store and in the apartment for another nine years after that day before being released to sell and go on with what God wanted in my life! God knew what was best for me. I didn't, but thought I did. I had to wait another nine years. Nine years, I just had to trust God. I felt that He had tricked me, but He made sure I was well looked after and that I had a beautiful apartment where I could live until He was ready to move me on.

Again I became restless and bored. God had made me very aware that I could not handle men very well (which I didn't agree with, I felt I could handle them). I told God that I was nice to men and that I didn't understand what He was talking about. It didn't take long before He answered me. "Child, you have this thin veneer of being nice to men, but underneath it you watch for their weak spots and attack." God has a way of telling you the truth about you, and there is no point in protesting because He is always *right*. I told God, "Right now, I am sure I can date, and don't worry about me. I'll just go on a date and leave them at the door, and that is it." I can do this (please note the "I" thing is back again). The "I" thing is an attitude that comes from ego, and people who experience this are determined to do things their way, and they stop listening to God. So, I was having an "I" moment. I am such a slow learner because so many times I did this "I" thing, and I just didn't get how being absorbed in ego can disconnect you from God.

I felt quite pleased with myself discussing dating with God and telling Him that I was going to do this. (I was being stubborn and ignoring God's wisdom). The next day, I was working at the meat counter when this little old man came into the store. The two girls serving behind the counter knew him. As far as I knew, I had never seen him before. He was five feet nothing and at least eighty years old. He was wearing a dirty old raincoat and shuffled when he walked. Now back to the meat counter where I was.

He ordered some lunch meat, and the conversation between the two of us went something like this:

"How's your husband?" he asked.

"We are divorced," I replied.

"I'm sorry."

"I am not."

He asked me again the same question. "How is your husband doing?"

"I don't keep track of my ex-husbands," I said.

He then said, "I live with my brother, and we go dancing most Saturdays."

"Well, good for you," I replied sarcastically.

The two girls at the front of the store were killing themselves with laughter and watching us. I wondered why. Then he said, "I would love to take you dancing this Saturday."

I looked at him and said, "Why?" I thought, *This man is no Mel Gibson* (how rude of me). He left the store, and I never saw him again.

The girls said I had missed the chance of a lifetime of marrying into money because he and his brother were rich chicken farmers known throughout the area. Here was God "showing me" what I was capable of dating. I was nowhere near ready to handle dating. To go on dates now would really mess everything up. I also would have undone all the good work God had done with me so far. My pride was hurt. I thought, *How dare you do this to me, God!* In the end, I had to laugh at what God was doing; He has such a sense of humor.

The girls teased me about it for weeks after, and I was sick of hearing about it. I left dating alone after that incident for a while. A similar incident happened again soon after this, which my daughter remembered. Same scenario, but the man interested in me was a wimpy stamp collector. Again in my subtle rude way, I spoke to him, and he also shuffled off, never to be seen again.

God was really being my Father, a real Father to me. Calming down after the date incidents, I felt bad about the way I had treated the men who wanted to date me. No question about it, I had snubbed them, but life goes on. Does God really do this stuff to you? Yes, He does. Make sure you praise and thank Him for doing it as well. Everything works in God's timing, not ours.

I must confess that I had a double-barreled shotgun, which I knew how to load and use and had all the shells I needed. At night, I was always alone in my apartment above the store. If anyone broke in at night, there was only one staircase they would have to come up to reach the apartment and me. I was not going to take any chances, so if I am at the top of the stairs with the shotgun, I would not miss you. The girls who worked for me were horrified, but it wasn't them alone every single night. They had husbands and families to go home to. I had had my face smashed, I had been threatened, and there had been breakins, and my store was nearly burnt down with me in it. I felt vulnerable, so *"my time, my way."* It was no secret that I had the shotgun. I figured that that might help certain kinds of unwanted people stay away from the store after hours. If you visited me after the store was closed at ten in the evening, it would not be for a good thing. I learned how to shoot and load in the dark, and I was not messing about.

When my daughter came to live with me for a while while going to university, she too had a shotgun and could use it well. Again one night, we were broken into, and I told her to load the gun while the alarms were ringing and while I tried to get the police on the phone. I told her to, "Shoot anything that came up the stairs." "Mom, I can't, they are people!" she said. My reply was, "No, they are not. They are ducks without feathers." I had had it with a lot of things. The thieves left without coming up the stairs. The police took forever to get to the store, and the thieves were never caught, anyway. I spoke to the volunteer fire chief a couple of days later, asking how much the fine was when you call in and it is a false alarm. He asked me, "Why?" And I said, "I am not waiting for the police to get here if I ever get broken into again. I need a quicker response. You guys answer in minutes, not hours." He asked me, "You don't cook do you, Gloria?" "No," I said. "So call in and say it is a grease fire so that we will know it is a break-in." Hallelujah! It was arranged. I had a backup plan.

Another time when I was alone, in the middle of the night, there was a horrendous storm with lots of thunder and lightning. In the middle of this mess, the store alarm went off. It was hard to hear if anyone was moving around downstairs because of all the noise, plus the main alarm was going off. I loaded the gun and put spare shells in my pocket. What do I do next? Then I figured I will warn them that I am armed and will shoot. There were huge timber beams in the apartment. I pointed the gun to the floor where the beam was between the bedroom door and the living room and then fired one barrel. My ears were ringing, and the smell of gunpowder was everywhere. Then my nerves got me, and I had to go to the bathroom. Great! I sat on the toilet and loaded the gun, hoping they would not come up the stairs right then.

Guess what, the police this time arrived fast. We found out that the storm had set my alarm off. My life, ever so calm and serene, Ha! Meanwhile, people at the church were saying I should not have a gun and that I should trust the Lord more. My reply was, this is my life, and this is the way it is going to go. My priorities were God first (and I am still working on that), me second, and then the gun, and it is staying. The three of us together. And what does it say in the Bible about three strands? A cord of three strands can never be broken.

One year after the first Halloween incident when the store nearly burnt down, the church was still very unhappy with me having a shotgun. I was told I should get a guard for that night. I had invited some friends over, but they didn't make it. So, here I am home alone on another Halloween night. It was a very dark night, no moon. I was watching out of my window from upstairs about eleven thirty, and I saw three figures dressed in dark clothing and masks making their way to the back of my store. This was a sore spot, as that was where the fire was started last year, and still nobody had been charged for lighting it. I ran downstairs, double-checked the alarm, and then turned it off so I could go to the back of the store where the big steel door was. I could hear the guys tiptoeing around on the gravel on the other side of the door. Man, I had mixed emotions. Were these the guys who were there last year? *Take it easy, Gloria*, I told myself. I went back into the office and tried calling the neighbors. No luck. Then I tried the police but had to leave messages. Then I went back to the back door, and I could still hear them walking on the gravel. I was not sleepy. I went upstairs and loaded the gun and then unloaded it. If three guys were out the back, what were they up to? As far as I was concerned, they were up to no good!

No, I was not going out to see who was there with a baseball bat, but if I went out with a shotgun, I figured that would be different. I thought even if they had masks on, maybe I would still recognize one of them. I told myself to calm down and think it out. I went back into the office *again* and tried calling the neighbors and police again, but still no luck. Next plan, I will go out of the store but set the alarm so they couldn't get in if I was attacked. I then hid the key under a ledge by the front door. The plan was set; I had unloaded my gun, it was in my hand, and out I went!

I rushed out and heard a voice, "Drop the gun, lady. Now!" It didn't register with me that it was a policeman because they never get there on time, ever. I yelled back, "No, I am going to the back of the store to get the guys who are back there!" I ran around the side of the store with an unloaded shotgun in my hand, but the policeman didn't know that. As I ran around the store, I could see a police car parked with yet another policeman in it. The second policeman knew me. He told me that he didn't get the guys and that they had slipped away in the dark. The first policeman was yelling at me, and I was yelling back at him. The second policeman was trying to tell his partner that I was okay. I had given the second policeman the shotgun so he could see that it was not loaded, but the first policeman (who didn't know me) tried to say that I was crazy! I told him "No!" I had planned it well. What an uproar! The firemen were also out, and they came over to help settle things down. I got my gun back and went back in the store and thought sarcastically to myself, *Oh, what a quiet and peaceful night.* I wasn't charged with anything by the police, but the one policeman was so angry at me for disturbing the peace; he was still yelling at me. It was all like a three-ringed circus. Anyway, the policeman who knew me convinced his partner to back off, and I wasn't charged. I wanted out of that store so badly because I had so many bad memories; it just wasn't funny anymore.

Living in the village at that time was like living in the Wild West. Shoot first, or you will be shot! I was so upset and angry because here I am, a Christian, but nothing had settled down in my life yet. In fact, things were getting crazier. I was under constant attack by the demons who were saying they wanted me back because I was so special, but I knew that if I went back, I would have been ripped apart spiritually and physically and would not be in my body ever again. You just don't come back from hell. And now that I knew God, if I had gone back to the dark side, there would be no hope for me, no return trip. That is why it would be better for the demons if I would have died before my deliverance. Even better for them after the Lord saved me, I chose to go back to them. I shudder to think of that.

Later on that winter, a local married lady who liked to party without her husband told the local police she had been raped at the back of my store. I didn't believe it for one minute. I made some inquiries of my own as to where she might have been on that particular night. Sure enough, there was a place she had been partying where she should not have been. The guys there gave her booze and drugs, and the rest is history. The demons were always trying to give me and the store a bad name. Remember God showed me the store as a lighthouse. The atmosphere around the store was heavy. There would be stones and the like arranged in certain ways on the ground. Was it witchcraft voodoo or curses? It definitely was not from the Lord, and obviously these things were ill omens or curses so that I would have deep fear in my heart. I would pray over the inside of the store and would kick the stones and the other crap away and pray over the land all around the store. The Lord reminded me that I had previously put semiprecious stones in places on the inside of the store by the direction of the demons. God showed me where I had put them, and they were pulled out and destroyed.

Psalm 91:5 says, "You will not fear the terror of night, nor the arrow that flies by day, nor the pestilence that stalks in the darkness, nor the plague that destroys at midday. A thousand may fall at your side, ten thousand at your right hand, but it will not come near you."

Isaiah 49:24–26 says, "Who can snatch the plunder of war from the hands of a warrior? Who can demand that a tyrant let his captives go? But the LORD says, "The captives of warriors will be released, and the plunder of tyrants will be retrieved. For I will fight those who fight you, and I will save your children. I will feed your enemies with their own flesh They will be drunk with rivers of their own blood. All the world will know that I, the LORD am your Savior and Redeemer, the Mighty One of Israel."

God had all what was happening under His control.

CHAPTER 20

Why Do You Call Me a Witch?

L ife goes on. Two brothers tried to stab each other outside the store one night. I got between them and ended the fight. Another guy threatened to beat me up as he repeatedly did to his girlfriend. He was always drunk and on drugs. One night when the store had closed, it was cold and dark, and three young guys whom I knew were drunk and hovering outside my store. One of the three had kicked his foot against a steel pole, and his foot was bleeding. His friends asked if I would put a bandage on his foot, so I went into the store, locked the door behind me, and brought out some bandages. As I was doing this, another guy came up behind me and started to cuss at me and threaten me. The three other guys said they would help me, but I didn't think so; they were too inebriated. The older guy was threatening to beat me up. Looking right into his eyes, I told him if he so much as touched me, I would sue him. What was inside of him hated me. All I could see when I looked in his eyes was pure evil and hate for me.

A neighbor heard the commotion and called the police. When I told the police sergeant about what happened and that I wanted this man to be charged for threatening me, etc., he said he couldn't charge the man. I asked why, and the sergeant told me that it wouldn't stand up in court because I had stood up to him. That would have been viewed as me egging the guy on. Can you believe this? So, I couldn't charge him for threatening me. I still wanted it in the officer's report in case he tried to harm me again later. This guy was going to kill me, he had such hate in his eyes. I stood up to him, which just infuriated him even more. Who was looking after me? Jesus was my bodyguard, though I didn't always see it this way. He really was.

Still going to church every Sunday. I was still crying whenever I got there. I always started to cry just before the sermon started and continued to cry until the end of the service. Arthur called me one evening to make sure I was coming to church on a particular Sunday because he and his wife had just ministered to a woman whose children were into Wicca (witchcraft). I believe they were twenty-three and twenty-five years old, a boy and a girl. Arthur and Angie thought that maybe I could take the mother out to lunch and share with her what God was doing in my life to help comfort and encourage her. I didn't see it being a problem, so I said yes. That Sunday, early in the morning, about two o'clock, there was freezing rain, and the roads were terrible. I got up at the usual time and heard the weather forecast. I looked outside and decided not to go to church that day.

I had totally forgotten about meeting the lady. My daughter was working on the computer, and it was about ten in the morning. I thought I was not going to church, so I decided to have a shower. I had a shower, and as I looked into the full-length mirror that was in the bathroom, on my stomach below my navel was the peace sign (the broken cross). The green veins showed against my white skin and really made this symbol stand out. This was *not what* I wanted to see on me! God hates this symbol, and I had it on *me*! I blinked my eyes, but it was still there. I rubbed it repeatedly with soap and water, but it was still there. I asked God to remove it, but it didn't disappear. I called my daughter in to the bathroom and asked her to look at my stomach and tell me what she saw. "Mom, that is the perverted peace symbol," she said without hesitation. Without a doubt, this dreadful thing was on my body!

In the midst of the turmoil, God came in to my mind and reminded me that I should be at church. Why? Because I am meeting the lady who has the children who are into witchcraft. To sum it up, I was now going to church, freezing weather or not. *Thank you, God, that the symbol is on my stomach and not my forehead. Nobody will see it, and it will likely be gone by tomorrow, right?* No, I was so wrong.

Quickly I got ready. I was praying in tongues the entire time. I beat all records for getting to church in London despite the weather and the roads being a disaster. God was with me, and that is all that mattered. As I was so late, I knew I would have to go to the back of the church parking lot to find a place to park. I would have to go uphill to park. The church was in a valley just below the parking lot. I quickly jumped out of my car and stopped. I was looking down on the dome of the church. I saw that there were angels fighting above it. Some were dressed in black, and some were in white. I watched, fascinated. The battle was fierce, and I could not tell who was winning.

A thought came to me, if such a battle is going on outside of the church, what is happening on the *inside* of the church? I knew I had to get inside as fast as I could. The path was so slippery, and it was slow-going. I wasn't always looking where I was going because I was watching the fighting going on above me. As I walked inside the church, it seemed very dark. Arthur was ushering that day and was just inside the door. The church was packed with people. I told Arthur what had happened to me with the peace symbol on my stomach. "Man, he is so very British and stodgy!" He said, looking very shocked, he didn't want to see what was on my stomach. I said, "I wasn't going to show it to you, anyway. I was just telling you about what had happened to me." He told me that there had just been an altar call.

It seemed to me that the church was in an uproar; it became so dark spiritually, even though there were bright lights everywhere. Arthur said that the lady had gone up for the altar call, and he told me to go up there and lay hands on her and pray for her. Good words, Arthur, but I didn't have a clue about who she was, and there were people everywhere and lots of people at the altar. *Help me, Lord. You brought me here, now what?* People were three deep at the altar. I looked around and only saw the backs of people. Then suddenly, I just saw the back of this lady, and I knew it was her. I pushed my way through, and I laid my hands on her. Instantly, she went down onto the floor. God said to me, "Don't take your hands off her until I tell you, my child." So, I knelt down beside her with both hands upon her body, praying in the spirit. I felt her temperature go sky high, and then so did mine. Somebody put their hand on my back, praying (later I found out it was Arthur), but he had to take his hands off me because of the heat radiating from both my body and the lady's.

What did God do for that lady at that time? I had no idea, and somehow I understood that it wasn't my place to know. I can tell you, though, that He took something away from her spiritually, something that she didn't need to have in her life. What was God's perspective on this incident? This was beyond my comprehension. I just stayed with her even after the altar call. We talked a lot even during the lunch in the church afterwards. She was asking me questions about what she could do for her children, and I told her how God was moving in my life and how God could bring her children out of Wicca (witchcraft) if that was their choice. I did not get home until late Sunday night. I felt quite sure that the peace symbol would be gone after the day I had, especially since I had been so obedient to God and in what He wanted me to do.

Not so! There it was, and it remained on me for about five years. I ended up getting used to having it there. I asked God many times to remove it. I would like to refer to a quote in the Bible that refers to a condition Paul had: "Three different times I begged the Lord to take it away. Each time he said, 'My grace is all you need. My power works best in weakness'" (2 Corinthians 12: 7–9). In my case I needed to remember what God had taken me out of. Over the years I forgot about the symbol on my stomach but not what God had done for me. I was very thankful that the symbol was under my clothing and, like I said before, not on the middle of my forehead. If you love God, Jesus, and the Holy Spirit, it has been my conviction not to purchase anything with this symbol on it either for myself or anyone else. It has always astonished me that even children's clothing has this symbol on it, and it's supposed to represent peace in our culture. Please pray and ask the Holy Spirit if it is acceptable to Him.

You really should. Have we been sleeping too long about these issues? Just think about it.

Still so many things were happening in my life. I was still learning. I still couldn't get over why He rescued me, so I asked Him. He replied, "By my grace, my child," and that is all He would say. It still blows me away. I was a done deal in my mind. Had I died, I would have gone straight to hell—no stopping, no second chances. God came straight into my life, pulled me out of an impossible spiritual situation, and kept me alive and well despite the number of times the enemy tried to sabotage me. All curses were broken in my life and in my children's lives. We had been set free, and free I was and am still today and forevermore. I wanted to somehow give back some of what God had done for me. I prayed to God this prayer, "Show me how you work, Lord. Show me when you release people from the enemy of their souls. Let me see your authority and power against all evil." And God has done this for me over and over again.

It is a strange thing; on the dark side, everybody I spoke to about spiritual "stuff" believed everything I said. Never was I called a witch or anything like it. Now that I was on the right side of the fence, so many people didn't believe that God had set me free, and I was called some interesting names, including a witch. They called me a witch in the present tense, like I was still in my past, and therefore unclean. Often other Christians made me feel unclean, which meant they didn't believe that Jesus had delivered me or that His blood was not powerful enough to keep me clean and believed I was still dangerous. What an insult to Christ who died for all our sins. But if people really believed in Christ and God and the Holy Spirit, they had nothing to fear from me, anyway. I spoke to my Heavenly Father about this and asked Him what good am I and what the point was of rescuing and restoring me. I am still an outsider looking in. Back came his answer, "Shelve it for now." So I did.

A great deal of Christians were very uncomfortable with hearing my testimony. They seemed scared of the occult and anything connected with it. By being scared of the occult, it actually gives the enemy a more powerful foothold because those Christians are denying the power of Christ to protect them in their lives. If you truly believe in Christ, you know that the Lord has you covered and protected, and nothing evil can touch you. Take my testimony as a good example, but you need to believe it, and you need to know whom you serve and mean it.

The Lord has often asked me to challenge people in churches. I will give you an example. I was giving my testimony at this particular church, and I knew that they were uncomfortable with my testimony. The Lord said to me to ask them if God had sent them fifty people such as I was before my deliverance, straight out of the occult, how would you as a church deal with those people? So, I did this, and there was a deathly silence. Your answer to that tells you how strong your walk with God is. Did Jesus not touch the demon-possessed? So then, can we do the same?

Then approximately one week later, this lady came into the store. She was about forty years old, blonde, six feet tall, built like a female amazon warrior, with a deep voice. She certainly caught my attention. She was dressed to suit her powerful personality, which was very striking. My nose twitched. I figured she was into something weird and that it wasn't of the Lord God. She spoke to me right away. Her husband was working in the area, and she was just looking around. She thought my store was very interesting, and bought some of the gift items. I knew she found me interesting, I didn't know why, I was just as curious and inquisitive about her. This woman came back a few times on different days, and the Holy Spirit was gently pushing me to speak to her about what was going on in my life and what I had come out of. I replied to the Holy Spirit, saying that was His job to do, not mine. I had been in enough trouble with people in general lately, so I didn't want to go there. Now the Holy Spirit is prodding me, not gentle pushing anymore, to speak to this woman.

A couple of weeks passed, and I didn't see her come back into the store, and then suddenly in she came. She had never been far away from my thoughts in those two weeks. Strangely, the store was not busy when she came in. We started to talk together, and I started to be obedient to what God wanted me to say. I spoke to her about God and what had happened in my life. When God speaks, we do not need to be challenging what He says. The response would be better to be humble and submissive so that His truth is revealed. In this case, I didn't want to talk to the woman coming into my store because I didn't think that it was my job. This woman was, in fact, a "satanic priestess." Now God was answering my question that I had asked earlier, remember? What was the point of rescuing and restoring me? She was my answer! I could talk to people who were in the occult and they would know I had been there. God you are so good.

I told this woman that I was now involved with Christians. She came back, saying, "I cannot stand Christians!" My reply was, "Neither could I until I had been delivered." Then ever so lightly, we touched on the subject of God. She told me about her powers. I asked her, "How old are you?" She told me she was forty. I told her she would be lucky to be coherent by the time she was fifty. Why? I told her that what was inside her was not her own power, but *"its"* *power* (the demon she had inside of her). I told her that it will keep on using her, and when your body and brain are past their usefulness, you could go mad or have a heart attack or maybe a stroke. Then you just might overdose on drugs. You don't see it now, but you are in *bondage*! The Lord showed me her life, and I recognized some things in her that were all too familiar to me and my previous experiences. Startled and almost afraid, she disagreed with me; I found it interesting that she was scared of me, or was it what was inside of me, Jesus Christ. I told her, "That is fine, but you have been warned." It was still not over between her and me. I walked her to her car carrying her groceries, and then out of my mouth, here it came (not my doing, I might add), "You are in the occult." "Yes," she replied, "And you were, were you not?" "Yes," I replied. Here God was showing me just how useful I could be. The Holy Spirit came down and flooded that whole area around her car where we stood. We hugged each other, and she said, "Please pray for me." And I did right there on the spot. I prayed for her daily as led by my Lord. I wasn't sure that I would ever see her again as she drove away.

A month later, she came back again. She told me that her brother in Calgary was a warlock, and she was afraid that they were going to kill him for being disobedient to his cult. She then proceeded to tell me that her spirit guides had told her not to contact me ever again, or else she would be stripped of her powers. I said, "So why are you here?" Her reply was, "I am so drawn to you. Please keep me in your thoughts and prayers." She then said, "I am a high satanic priestess of an occult order in London. If you knew all I could do, you would be terribly afraid and would not speak to me, and you would avoid me." My reply was, "God had taken me out of what you are into, and so I am not afraid. I can only say that the Lord wants to take you out of this as well. Why did he bring you here? Why are you back here to speak to me again? Our backgrounds are similar but not the same, and you know and see that something marvelous has happened to me in the spiritual. I am out of bondage, while you are deep in bondage." She said, "I have to go. I have had enough talk about God." This woman was really searching.

I never saw her again. I prayed for her for almost a year and then stopped. God showed me that despite my past, He could use me for His glory against the enemy. No matter what people said about my past, Jesus had my back, and I was His. Did the priestess make it? I have no idea, but she touched my heart.

CHAPTER 21

Where Does My Help Come From?

y store manager and I had arranged to go on a shopping trip for the store in Toronto. Everything was arranged, she would be at the store at six thirty in the morning to pick me up. Well, I didn't require an alarm clock that morning—*Crash*! *Crash*! *Bang*!— time: six o'clock. There was the sound of breaking glass; something large had been broken downstairs in the store. I was up in the bathroom. My thought was, had May broken the glass in the front door by accident? How wrong I was. I flew downstairs, the alarm now going off, and saw that two men had broken into the store! I was in the doorway of the office, and they both saw me and had masks on. One picked up a crowbar and came up the stairs swinging the crowbar at me as he came forward. There I was backing up, looking at him as he was swinging at my face. The police later counted seventeen times where he hit the wall in his attempt to hit me.

His partner called him, he turned, and I turned and ran back upstairs. I opened the bedroom window, yelling, but no one could hear me with the alarm system going. My phone would not work upstairs in the bedroom, so down I went again. I could hear them walking on all the broken glass. I connected on the phone with the police, and they were on their way. There was a truck right outside the store door and a restaurant just up the road. The people in there could see what was happening, yet nobody came to help me.

The robbers stole all the cartons of cigarettes. In their haste, they had dropped one of the bags full of cigarettes and left fast. The police arrived, and so did everyone else, including the truck driver and the people in the restaurant. So much for good neighbors. I phoned May and warned her not to come in. To make a long tedious story short, as always, the thieves were never caught. I felt like I had been raped. Just as with the fire, I felt so very alone. Where was God, Jesus, and the Holy Spirit? The enemy was definitely there. So, I nearly had my face broken again, but for what? So, the enemy could give themselves a medal, saying they had hurt me again. I tried working in the store that day to take my mind off things, but it wasn't a good idea. A customer came in and made a stupid joke about the incident, and I lost it. I went up one side of him and down the other. He was then upset with me because I yelled at him. He didn't know how near I came to hitting him with something extremely hard. I wanted people to hurt as much as I was hurting. What was creepy was I started to withdraw, and I became scared, looking at every male customer who came into the store after this attack. I was wondering, was it him or them? I felt so insecure and unsafe, and I couldn't get the incident out of my mind.

That night after closing the store, my nerves were not good. My relationship with God was in bits. I called the devil and his tribe of demons everything I could think of. I felt it necessary to go down into the store and try to worship the Lord as I always did. I would play my CD player at the back of the butcher area and share my heart with him. With worship music playing, I sat down on a Silverwood's plastic milk carton and cried and cried. What else would I have to face? How much more could I take? Only the night light was on at the back of the store, and it was just over my head. The door at the front was boarded up. Suddenly, as I sat there, I could feel a draft, and it was moving my hair. My eyes looked down at the floor, and there were shadows. Things with wings were flying above me. I could not have cared less; I was numb.

I said out loud, "If you demons are trying to frighten me and drive me mad, go for it because it will take a lot more than this to drive me insane!" I yelled that out to the air around me. "So, give it your best shot and show yourselves. Come on, you cowards! Let me see you and let us see what happens." Guess what, nothing happened, absolutely *nothing*! I packed up the worship and went upstairs to bed. As I was getting into bed, something a lot heavier than I got into the bed beside me. I felt the bed go right down on the other side of me. I laughed and said to the invisible thing, "So, you are still trying your luck to frighten me. Go for it, do it." What I said next is unprintable. I felt abandoned and at the mercy of everything that thought it could take me apart. I said to it, "Well, do it and get it over with now!"

I either fell asleep or passed out, I am not sure. Then Jesus called my name, "Gloria." "Yes, Lord," I replied as I sat up in bed. The time was two in the morning. Jesus was standing at the end of my bed. It was definitely Jesus. He spoke Psalm 23 to me. Jesus said, "Gloria, I am your shepherd. You will not be in want. I will make you lie down in green pastures and lead you beside still waters and will restore your soul. I will guide you in paths of righteousness for my name's sake. Even though you walk through the valley of the shadow of death, you will fear no evil, for I am with you. My rod and staff will comfort you. I will prepare a table before you in the presence of your enemies. I will anoint your head with oil, your cup will overflow. Surely goodness and love will follow you all the days of your life, and you will dwell in my house—forever." Such a peace came over me. I was safe. I didn't have to try to convince myself that I was really safe. I fell back to a peaceful sleep.

Just before going back to sleep on the fateful night, however, Jesus took me back in a vision to the evening when I was in the store downstairs when the demons were flying over my head. His hand was just above my head. Nothing was going to touch me there. Then when I went upstairs to go to bed, Jesus had his arm between me and the thing that was lying in bed with me. So, nothing was going to touch me there either. Can you believe this? How great is our God. I just wished I had seen Jesus before I saw those other evil things flying around me. "Never let me go, Lord," I prayed. "Never." I fell into a much-needed sleep.

The Holy Spirit was urging me to be more hospitable and not so hostile towards other people. My birthday was coming up, and my daughter gave me a gift all nicely wrapped up. I opened it, and it was a book called *Christian Hospitality*. I thought how God never misses a beat, amazed at how He so effectively uses other people to accomplish His purposes in our lives. "Why did you buy me this book?" I asked her. "Because you are ready for this, Mom," she said. She was just being obedient to what was laid on her heart, and she wasn't even Christian. God uses all people. Remember, if you don't listen to God speaking to you, He will make sure someone else speaks what He wants into your life. It stops you in your tracks. It may be difficult to believe that God does these things, but bless Him, He does.

Christmas was coming, so with Darice saying she would help me (unheard of for me the person who doesn't cook), I invited thirteen people for Christmas. First, I had to buy pots and pans, knives and forks, as the ones I used to have I had given away a long time ago. For the last few years, I used paper plates and plastic knives and forks for utensils and wouldn't cook. Darice said, "Mom, we are not going to eat off paper plates. Use plastic cutlery. If you are doing this for God, let us do it right!"

"Okay, Okay," I said. I also bought china for the event. Just look at what God was doing in my life. He was gradually transforming me into a "regular" person, doing whatever regular people do. He was doing this despite my protest, moaning, and groaning.

God was molding me into what He had created me to be. He was restoring me. I could now move on in my life in Him and actually have a life. I was finally not being a puppet, not masquerading a part like I did before. There are so many aspects of my life I found difficult to understand. As for me, I am sticking like glue with God, as I know He will always show me the right way to go.

So, here we go, thirteen people for Christmas dinner on Christmas day. My daughter and I invited a Filipino woman married to an English man and three of their children. I also invited some other young Filipino girls. Now it is the day before Christmas Eve. I had gotten up as normal to get ready for work, and then suddenly I fell down the step from the bedroom. I hit the wall hard and twisted my ankle. My daughter was asleep in the room next door and hardly heard a thing. I didn't need this because the store would be very busy and busier with organizing gift and fruit baskets. I phoned the staff to see if someone could take my place for a while. I found someone else to work the store for me.

The next day, my ankle and leg were not in good shape, and I was not able to drive to hospital. I phoned around and asked if anyone can take me to emergency since I thought I had broken it. Christmas was the next day. There was a taxi service out of Melbourne, but all cars were busy. Everybody was busy, and my daughter would not be home until late that night. Don't ask me where the thought came from, but I called my friend, Mike, in London.

Coincidence or not, he was home with his son, and he was happy to take me. So, he had to drive all the way out to Melbourne to pick me up and then take me to the hospital. When he arrived, off we went, my ankle and leg now really hurting. The hospital X-rayed it, put it in a splint, bandaged it up, and gave me pain pills and crutches. The three of us had a great time. God was putting us together. I treated them to supper for taking me into London. It was a good time, bad ankle and everything. He dropped me back at the store, crutches and all. I had to go up the stairs on my butt. Slow, slow, and slower.

When Mike took me to the hospital, he said he had not received a check from his work, and therefore he had not been able to buy presents for his wife and children. God touched my heart, and I said, "Okay, pick things out from the store. I will put them on a bill for you and pay me when you receive the check. At the same time, I invited him to Christmas dinner. Next morning, obviously I would not be cooking because of my leg. Darice jokingly said I had done it all on purpose so I wouldn't have to do anything. She volunteered Mike to come and help with the Christmas dinner preparations. God was there. The guests arrived, and everything went well. No one wanted to leave. We were all singing, and the guitar was playing. The whole day was a huge success, and who planned it? God.

I still had trouble with men. I had been married and divorced twice now. I really did not respect men; in fact, I silently hated them and didn't trust them. I even felt the demons were male. They were not any particular sex in reality, but I saw them as male. I had had problems with my earthly mother and father, and I also struggled with God being a male figure. I knew within myself there was still a pile of residue, garbage, and problems that needed to come out of me. I had a lot of hurt and bitterness that needed to be healed, and God can not heal that just overnight. The way I looked at this was God first and then me. Bypass men and I won't have any problems. I could not have been more wrong!

One day, a young man who worked for me as a part-time butcher out of nowhere came up to me (in the store) and said, "Gloria, you are not a respecter of men." I stood there for a moment, shocked, and then turned and walked away, my mind working overtime with his remark. I am not a respecter of men, how dare he say that about me. I turned and went back to where he was standing and gave him more than a piece of my mind. How dare he say that? I felt good about telling him off and then walked away again, feeling quite smug and self-satisfied with *me*!

For the next two weeks, the words, "You are not a respecter of men," kept coming up within me just like a bad dose of acid reflux and heartburn, only I could not take the pills for it. Then I got it—the lightbulb went on. I needed an attitude adjustment where men were concerned. Two weeks later, I apologized to him for my behavior. He didn't even remember what he had said. God certainly knew where I needed adjusting. At a time when I just knew Mike (my current husband) as a friend, and nothing was going on between us, neither of us had ever thought there was anything in the works with regards to a relationship together. I got this phone call from him, asking me if I could loan him $750. My back went up; I am not in the habit of loaning people money. Frankly, it is not a good practice and one I was *not* getting involved in. You lose friends and make enemies when money is involved in dealings. So, I did the Christian thing, told him I would pray about it and get back to him. In my mind, though, I was saying, "Sorry, buddy. No deal." That was the way I dealt with the problem. Money was a tender subject for me, especially when it concerned *men*!

Then God spoke to me. "Gloria, I want you to loan him this money." I told the Lord that this was not a good idea. Mike had a bad reputation for always being broke, and I didn't trust him to pay it back, so it was better for me to agree not to do this. God said, "Gloria, I own everything in this world, and that includes the store and everything in it."

"The money isn't really yours."

"You are my steward of what has been given you. Loan him the money."

This was not what I wanted to hear. This whole incident was making me feel annoyed and upset. *Why do I have to deal with it at all? It is Mike's problem, not mine! He was always having money problems. God, don't make them mine!*

I told Mike I was still praying about it (liar) and left it for a few more days, trying to think how I could wriggle out of this situation. I didn't want to be obedient, I didn't want to loan him the money. Then God turned the pressure up in me. Again, I am at the crossroads. Make sure you make the right decision, Gloria. This is another test. So, reluctantly I caved and loaned Mike the money. I printed out an IOU for $750 and made sure Mike signed on the dotted line. Looking back, I have to laugh because God never told me at the time that this would be my future husband. I was being very bossy and not very kind either. Fred divorced me August, 1991. Michael and I were married, June 1995.

Meanwhile, I am hearing from Christian friends saying once you loan a fellow Christian money, you should *not* expect it back. Really, I thought, that is *not* how I see it. Mike asked for a loan, and I gave him the loan. The agreement was that he would pay it back. It had nothing to do with being Christian. A loan was a loan, and after all, I wasn't charging interest, *so there!*

The fun continues. Several weeks went by, and then the Lord spoke to me yet again. "Gloria, this is a forgivable loan, repayment is not necessary." The scriptures say the generosity towards those in need remains pleasing to God. "Give freely without begrudging it, and the LORD your God will bless you in everything you do. There will always be among you who are poor. That is why I am commanding you to share your resources freely with the poor and with other Israelites in need." (Deuteronomy 15:10-11 Life Application Bible). Again, it was brought home to me that I was simply a steward charged with wise distribution of things God had entrusted in my care, as all I have belongs to the Lord. (I didn't even know that this guy was going to be my husband.)

It was a struggle for me to be obedient and let it go. Each Christian is to give cheerfully. I was not there yet. I looked up the word *cheerful*. It states, "Showing in their behaviors that they are happy and joyful." This was definitely *not* happening. Okay, here we go again. It took another few days before I could talk to Mike and tell him that the Lord had spoken to me and said that the loan was forgiven. Mike thanked me. I said, "Thank God." Help me, Lord, on these issues.

Mike lived in a big city, and I lived in small town, about half-an-hour drive apart. We had different friends and went to different churches. He was still married when I met him, although his wife had left him. He loved his wife and wanted to get back with her. All of his friends would tell you how at Easter, Christmas, or New Year's Mike would be depressed and down because none of his family were around, not even his wife or his children. There was a husband-and-wife team out of my church who were mentoring us separately. So, we often would bump into each other at their house.

For a long time, I had no idea that Mike was twelve years younger than I was. I thought that we were about the same age. A couple of strange things had happened between us. I had been by myself for four years, and I figured that I would remain single for the rest of my life. People and friends from the church would say, "Gloria, we can see you marrying a pastor." Even if that were to come true, that really did not appeal to me in any way whatsoever. Besides, God was not saying anything of the sort, and so I left it. The Lord would sometimes give Mike and me a word for each other.

Mike rented a townhouse in London, and often there would be home church meetings (or Bible studies) there. I was often invited, and often I didn't go. We were bumping into each other at church functions and other gatherings and had no problem chatting together. I knew that Mike was in debt. He worked for himself and had spent a chunk of money trying to get back with his wife. They went to marriage counselors in London, and they had counseling from a pastor at a church. He also tried to invest some money wisely to impress his wife, but he lost it all. It was not a very happy situation, but he was dealing with it with the Lord. He also had his own group of close friends, so I didn't think he was lonely.

So many strange spiritual things were still happening in my life. If only there was a can of some kind of spray that you could eliminate those odorous horrible spiritual beings, just spray them, and they would be gone! Not so, one step at a time, in hand with the Lord. One time, I was in bed in my apartment late one night, and the phone rang. It was Mike. Even over the phone, I knew he was acting strange. He was talking about his wife and was going over to her house to "save" her. His voice even changed and became very deep and raspy. My CD player, which was in my room playing Christian music, slowed down and sounded awful. My room became extremely cold all of a sudden. I cried out, "Help, Lord." The Lord replied, "Keep calling him Michael and start saying the Psalms I give you out loud." I still had Mike on the phone. I knew something really spiritually weird was happening.

I had no problem doing this, but things seemed to be getting out of hand fast. I said, "Lord, stay with us!" and He did. To me, it wasn't Michael talking on the phone anymore. If Mike had not been talking about his wife, I would have just cut the conversation fast. I knew he was in trouble and knew he shouldn't go over and see his wife because she would freak out. I told him this. I remember being very calm but also feeling very cold. I was freezing but following the Lord's instructions. Then it seemed Mike dropped the phone, and it sounded as if he was rolling around on the floor. The Lord told me to just keep saying the Psalms.

I now had to turn off my CD player, as it was now making screaming noises. I pulled the plug right out of the wall. There was a very unpleasant odor in my room. Guess what, I had uninvited guests (demons) again. Mike had picked up the phone again, and in the same horrible voice, he told me he was going to visit his wife. And again, I tried to tell him that that was not a good idea. He just dropped the phone, and I heard a door slam on the other end of the phone.

I prayed and prayed. My room was like an iceberg. The CD still wouldn't work, and the bulb in the lamp beside my bed decided to explode. Fortunately, I had a flashlight in my drawer. It was far too late to call anybody for help, so I just kept doing what the Lord had said, "Read the Psalms." Then I went downstairs, got a hot drink and hot water bottle, went to bed, and fell asleep. Something touched me and woke me up and said, "Get pen and paper. We want you to write." I put the other bedside light on. Voices were coming at me, telling me what to write. One spoke. "You and Mike will marry. There is a need for you to both start your relationship *Now*. There will be no waiting until you are married." It talked sexually and then said, "*We* will bless this union." Whatever was around me at the time, I believed everything it said. It had such charisma. The atmosphere was thick and heavy. I felt drugged.

So, I put the note in my drawer. I then passed out. Jesus called my name, "Gloria." "Yes, Lord." "*Take out that note and burn it now!* Flush the ashes down the toilet, leave nothing of it behind." I was somewhat confused. You better believe it, but I knew Jesus's voice. I didn't know the first voice that was from hell. This time, my mind was clear, and I did what Jesus said, and the note was destroyed. I tried to phone Mike. You may ask why. Well, if all this was happening to me, what was happening to him? Unfortunately, I was still getting the busy signal, so the phone was still off the hook. Guess what, I didn't sleep for the rest of the night.

The next day, I was going to a Christian business meeting in downtown London. I felt very unclean with what had happened to me. I also felt very concerned about Mike because he was so not in his right mind when he phoned me the night before. The meeting was early, and we had breakfast first. I still had no contact with Mike, and then I saw two of his friends at the business breakfast. They were sitting at a table just across from me. I asked them, "Have you heard from Mike at all?" "Yes," they replied. Great! They knew what had happened to him. He had gone to his wife's house first, which was bad news, and then he took his van somewhere and ran out of gas. He was under a demonic attack. He had a total spiritual meltdown. His friends had found him in a mess, and he was now home and safe. "Thank you, Lord."

The lady I was with at the breakfast table, who also went to the same church as I did, looked at me and said, "What is your interest in him?" "He is a friend," I replied. She asked me, "Are you sleeping with him?" Shocked, I gave her a look and said, "How dare you say that, absolutely not. And how absurd that you would even think that." *Please someone tell me what is going on because God definitely isn't telling me*, I thought. Why was the enemy interested spiritually in myself and Mike? We were two nobodies. We were just ants in dinosaur country. I remember saying to the Lord, "If you ever do put me with someone, their background would have to be as weird as mine." Who would be able to understand me? Not too many people. I figuratively wiped my hands and said there is no chance of that happening.

Not understanding it then, I now realize the demons knew that God was going to put us together, so if they could put us together first, it would be out of God's timing, and it would be wrong and totally disastrous to whatever God may call us to do. Plus, we would be dishonoring Him, the one who had done so much for us. As fast as the demons were determined to shipwreck God's plans, God was quietly working even faster to keep everything on track, His track. Mike and I, the two ants, didn't have a clue to what exactly was going on yet! I didn't see Mike when he was going through his weird spiritual meltdown. I was warned by certain churches to have absolutely no contact with him. I was told that he was banished from their assemblies until further notice. Why? I asked myself?

Here was a man in trouble, and no one came to help him. Everybody was saying, "Leave him be." I was told to not talk to him by phone or letter. I thought, did this guy have leprosy? Are the churches not supposed to help their brothers in Christ? For what happens to the smallest piece in the body is felt by the whole body in Christ, is it not? I was not impressed with how these Christians were treating Michael. How come so many churches profess to be shepherds to their people but allow the wolves of hell to scatter their sheep? God, on the other hand, said, "When Mike phones you, call him by his name Michael. No matter what he talks about or how he sounds, talk to him as you would have before he became sick."

When he did call, the spiritual tension on the phone between Mike and myself was not good, and I can only describe it as a high-voltage electrical current—touched in the wrong place it could harm and damage you. I did as the Lord told me. As long as I knew God was in the middle of all this, I was not going to make it a problem or have any fear. Furthermore, I didn't listen to my Christian friends who told me not to talk with Michael. Demons, unholy spirits, evil entities, and the like, I tell you my God reigns over all of them!

Mike was out of it for about four weeks. The people closest to Mike had thought he had lost his mind. The demons tried to make him think that he was Jesus. His wife and pastor wanted to put him in an asylum. His brother and sister came over from Ireland and tried to take him home with them. It was all a horrible dark spiritual mess. The church wanted to bury him alive, as he was an embarrassment to them. Why? you might ask. Well, he had given his life to the Lord. I thought, so what would they have done with me if they had seen me at my worst? Didn't they realize that God was watching all that goes on? Again, I just had to be careful because I felt it was all my fault. Guilt was rising fast. No! I will not accept this. God Himself has directed me on what to do. God Himself would be in charge of the outcome.

Why I was feeling guilty was because a few weeks prior, I had had meetings with Tammy who definitely had a host of demons within her. Demons don't display hospitality; they show hostility and hatred. I had asked Mike and his friend to pray against what was coming against her. I thought it was me that was the cause of Mike's distress, and I should never have involved him or his friend in this matter. There was no doubt in my mind Mike went through a horrifying, unclean spiritual experience. I was also remembering the guy who had hung himself the night I was with Alex, and look what happened to him.

When I think about it now, I do not think my actions had *anything to do with* Mike's meltdown, but I really had concern for him because I could relate to what he was going through, and no one, Christian or otherwise, was standing by him that I could see.

CHAPTER 22

Who Is Spiritually Unclean?

Mike and I were in the stages of developing a good friendship. He was a very honest person. Maybe he was too honest for some people to take. People tended to judge him because of his honesty. Michael was recently separated from his wife when I met him, and shortly after that, he was divorced. However, he desperately wanted to make the marriage work. He did everything he could to try to get her back, but his wife was not interested. So, to impress his wife, he invested some money he had into a venture that failed, and he lost all of his money. It seemed that all of his efforts backfired, and the people around him saw him as a bit of a loser with the exception of just a few. He then tried everything he could to stay connected to his children, especially his youngest son, who still lived with his mother. Mike loved the Lord, and he was also trying to find himself through the Lord at the time I met him. He never lied about his situation. He was brutally honest about his failed marriage and about the fact that he was in debt. All of his efforts at that time seemed to go nowhere.

The adventures of being a young Christian continued. Mike and I had been invited to a house church in London. It was not a large group of people. They were giving testimonies of what God had done in their lives. Here we met a young man whom the group were grooming to be a "prophet." Really, what kind of prophet? I wondered to myself. Was he God's prophet or something else's prophet? I was not sure about that, I didn't get a good feeling about the group. When we were talking with him, he said he could lay his hands on people and draw their energy out, making it his own. Only he didn't tell people what he was doing when he did this. This was not of God, my spirit cried out. This was very unclean. Who or what was training him?

He said that he could travel to the heavens, where he would walk among the spirits, looking for Jesus, and he needed to find the real Jesus, as there were many spirits by that name. Mike and I really didn't feel comfortable with this at all. There were a couple of other strange things going on with this man as well. The people in this house group were proud of what they viewed as their 'prophet'. They then told us about another man who was considered to be a "higher prophet" by this group, and they wanted us to meet him. A meeting was arranged but praise the Lord we never made it to that meeting. This smelt like all the "stuff" my mother and grandmother had been into. None of it was God-inspired or holy.

I phoned the lady in charge of the house church, and as gently as I could, I told her that her group had best pray for this young prophet they claimed as "theirs," as this was not God at work but the devil. I told her that this young man needed good spiritual help and a deliverance as well as the higher prophet whom we had not met yet. She then verbally attacked me over the phone. She called me a witch and evil, among many other things. I put the phone down, called Mike, and told him what had happened. He then phoned the lady, telling her that she should be asking God about these things, as they were not spiritually correct. Then she phoned this pastor who knew Mike, but exactly what she told him didn't come out until a few days later.

So, a couple of days later, I had a weekly church meeting at my apartment. All of the regular people were there, including this pastor. At about halfway through the evening, the pastor told me in no uncertain terms that I should be careful how I speak to people about things I didn't know anything about. He also said that I could be unclean spiritually. He was obviously referring to the conversation I had had with this lady a couple of nights ago. This upset me because where was his discernment? Here is a pastor who really didn't know this woman who complained about me, and he really didn't know me either. I was shocked that he believed everything this woman had said about me. She had gone to see him where he worked. Never once did the pastor check with God, Jesus, or the Holy Spirit, and he didn't even check the facts with me either.

I told him, "The group was out of line with the Lord, and the pastor had better be asking the Lord what was going on and not asking and believing other people!" There were five single girls in our group at my apartment that night. They spoke up and said how they had not felt comfortable around this woman and how they didn't trust her or the rest of the group. This shut the pastor up, as they were part of his flock. I must confess that there was no love lost between this pastor and myself at this time. About a week later, Mike and I left from his townhouse to go to Guelph. We found out later that this woman had come to Mike's townhouse to have a word with me about my words of caution over "their" prophet; they were going to put me in my place. The Lord made sure I was not there when she arrived. After that, we had no more contact with that group.

Sadly, two years later, we met the young prophet on a street in London. He looked terrible. He told us he was slowly getting better after having a complete spiritual breakdown, and he no longer saw anyone in that group. Thank you, Lord, for your discernment in my life. My uncomfortable feelings about this group were proven correct.

Looking back on this incident about this woman and her group plus the two prophets, if you do not have Christ's discernment in your life, how easy it would be to slide into the dark side like this young man did. The enemy uses our egos to get in. Then trouble starts. If only this young man had prayed to the one and only God for the truth about his position, maybe then no madness or nervous breakdowns would have happened. He has become trapped in the wrong fisherman's net. Not every person who declared to be a Christian is truly a Christian.

"You believe that there is one God. Good! Even the demons believe that – and shudder." (James 2:19, Life Applications Study Bible).

That poor man had been used and abused first by the demons and then by the prophet and the group. Remember this group appeared Christian. He was deceived; if no true deliverance had taken place in his life after all this, he was still going to have multiple problems. Michael tried to stay in touch with him, but he just disappeared. We still prayed for him, never knowing the outcome of his life. "For we are not fighting against people made of flesh and blood, but against the evil rulers and authorities of the unseen world, against these mighty powers of darkness who rule this world, and against wicked spirits in the heavenly realms." (Ephesians 6:10-12 LASB)

At a later date came my second test concerning loaning money. It must have been about six months later when Mike phoned me again and explained that his work check had been delayed and that he would like to borrow $400 for just two weeks. The check he was waiting for should be in by then. Here we go again. So, I had (not God) already given him some money and forgave the loan as directed by the Lord and now a second loan! Here it comes, my stomach started to churn, is Mike hoping this one will be forgiven as well? I did not want to say yes, so I said I would phone him back. Back to the Lord I went with the question, and again God said I should loan Mike the money. My thinking was, okay, it was only for two weeks maximum no more freebies, and so it shouldn't be a big deal, right? I told Mike to come and pick the money up. I still wrote an IOU and had him sign it. I handed the money over to him, gave him a lecture stating that, "It must be back within the two-week period." Whose money is it, anyway? The first week went by no problem. By the second week, he had not even phoned, and I was not too happy. I wasn't even happy with the Lord, and he was not answering me or talking to me either. I phoned Mike and left him a message. "What am I *not* learning here?" I asked myself. "Help!" The money was due back on the Saturday, and it was now Thursday. I was getting anxious; I didn't believe that he would pay me back. Then suddenly, seemingly out of nowhere, Mike phoned and said he would be there on Saturday, probably early afternoon.

Okay, it was now Saturday, and I was working till ten that night. No sign of Michael or the money. It was now past ten, the store was closed, and still no sign of anybody or anything. I asked God, "Is this a punishment against me for not doing things correctly?" Was this being done deliberately? Was I feeling sorry for myself? Yes, I was. I was working myself up and getting distraught. I couldn't think clearly. I gave God a piece of my mind. I ripped into God about Michael. If God had not told me to loan him the money, none of this would have happened. From about ten thirty in the evening, God spoke to me after I calmed down enough to listen to what He had to say. He said I was to ask forgiveness of Him first because of my shenanigans, which I did, and then as soon as I had accomplished that, God said, "Now you must ask Michael for forgiveness for all the things you have attacked his character about." I was struck dumb.

Here I am at the crossroads again. Then there was a banging at the front door of the store. Time is eleven forty-five. It was Michael, and he actually handed me the money two minutes before midnight—the deadline for the money to come back. God was making sure that I would learn my lesson. I apologized to Michael and made him a cup of tea, and he left at about twelve thirty. His van had broken down, and that was why he had arrived late, and of course, he had to wait until it was fixed. The joke was on me. I must be a very slow learner. I do not like being tested. Could God help me here? Yes, he could, providing I let go of my pride and truly ask for His forgiveness for my attitude and spirit of disobedience. And He did. Just think, God knew this man was going to be my husband. Go figure! This would be my third marriage; the only difference was that God arranged this one.

PART 4

God and Mike's Proposal

CHAPTER 23

When God Tells You His Desire for Your Life

I was home alone after Christmas. It was around seven in the morning, and God called me. He said, "Gloria, get your Bible dictionary." I said, "Lord, I don't know where it is." "Go get it," He said. So, I hobbled over to where my books were and found it. I pulled it from the shelf, and very clearly God said to me, "I want you to look up two words—*dowry* and *betrothal*."

I read what it said about dowry. In the Middle East, the groom was expected to make a gift to his bride's father. The compensation to the father was not always paid in money. Jacob worked for seven years in order to marry Laban's daughter, Rachel. (Michael worked for the store for a year with no salary after we were married.) Women were not merely property to be purchased. The bride was also given gifts by her father, which she brought into the marriage.

The resources a woman brought into the marriage as a bridal gift remains hers, and this was very significant to me. (I brought the store into my marriage.) She was a property owner and an independent person who came into the relationship as a valued and valuable partner to her husband. I was impressed with this description of Hebrew marriage customs, and I wondered who this message was for.

Then came the explanation of betrothal. It means an engagement to marry. In Israelite times, there were two stages: 1) the betrothal and 2) a marriage ceremony a year later. A typical betrothal was a legal binding commitment. Even though the marriage was not consummated until after the actual wedding ceremony, only the man could break the betrothal by giving his betrothed a written certificate of divorce (Deuteronomy 24:1). As I studied these words, there was still nothing coming to me from my Father, so I asked, "Who is this word for, Lord?" Back came the answer loud and clear, "I want you to be betrothed to Michael." There was silence from me! Then stutter, stutter. I said, "This won't work, Lord. I hate men, and you know that! Mike owes a lot of money and wants to get back with his wife. What are you thinking, Lord? Marriage for me had never worked in the past, why would it work now?" I had so many doubts, so many misgivings.

Suddenly, I realized God's presence had left the room. He wasn't listening to me anymore. I love my Father dearly. Clearly, He had spoken strong words over me before, telling me that I was assertive and tenacious, just as He had created me to be. The way I had to look at the whole picture before God plonked this betrothal in front of me was that God was first in my life, me next, and then my children. Yet I knew I had a ton of problems inside of me all to do with men. I figured God would either take them away or work through them with me. Also, with the kind of life I had spiritually lived, it would take a man, at least, as weird as I was to make it work. So, beside God himself, I figured that I would be safe with my God, *no men!*

Yes, God loves his children. Yes! He has an awesome sense of humor. He can put things together that no men in their right minds can even think to put together and make it work. Then there is Michael and myself. Okay now, if I had received from my Father such a strong word, what had he given to Michael? Well, the day before, this is what had happened to Michael. He was spending the evening alone and was reading his Bible. The Lord told him to go to Isaiah chapter 6. He came to Isaiah chapter 6: 5-8.

> "Then I said, "It's all over! I am doomed, for
> I am a sinful man. I have filthy lips, and I live

among people with filthy lips. Yet I have seen the King, the LORD of Heaven' Armies. Then one of the seraphim flew to me with a burning coal he had taken from the altar with a pair of tongs. He touched my lips with it and said, "See, this coal has touched your lips. Now your guilt is removed and your sins are forgiven." Then I heard the Lord asking, "Whom shall I send as a messenger to these people? Who will go for us?" I said, "Here I am. Send me".

Mike said to God, "Here I am send me."

God said to Mike, "I want you to marry Gloria." When Mike received this message, he sat in silence for some time. Then he responded, and his one thought was, *I am going to have to test the spirits to be sure that this was indeed from God.* Then Mike said to God, "Lord, if you really want me to do this, have Gloria phone me in the morning first thing." He then wiped his hands of it and went to bed, figuring that was the end of that.

Oh, what fun! I phoned Mike the next day in the morning, wondering if he had received any message from God. Just think about this—Mike sort of knew what was going on because he received his message the night before. I received my message the next morning. God definitely knew what was going on. I fished around, asking Mike if God had given a word to him about anything. Mike went around and around the mulberry bush. "Yes," he said, "Sort of." He told me a bit of this and a bit of that. Then I lied, and I said that God had told me that we would be in ministry together for about a year. Mike replied that he had no problem with that. We were both skirting around the message clearly given to us by God. Then somehow it all came out, what God had really wanted was for the two of us to be joined together in marriage under Him!

I was scared silly. I had a real negative attitude, wondering how it could possibly work. Did God really know what He was doing? I had so many mixed emotions; my mind was a minefield. As for Michael, I didn't have a clue what he was thinking. I was busy looking after me and not doing a good job at that either. Mike was say-ing that we should start telling people about becoming engaged. My answer was no! I didn't need to have anxiety about this matter.

At the same time, I knew I needed to tell my daughter, Darice. On the day I wanted to tell her, she was having a shower. So, in I went and said to her, "Darice, I have something to tell you." She said, "What is it, Mom?" I just couldn't spit it out. She insisted. "What is it? Tell me!" I still couldn't tell her. She then said, "Well, I know what it is." "You do?" I replied. "Yep, you are going to marry Mike." "How did you know that?" I asked. "Mom, I just thought of the worst thing you could do concerning men, and that was it." What could I say after that? I was at a loss for words.

Mike and I both had a sense that God wanted us to join in marriage. The idea of marriage settled into our being, I wanted to tell Arthur and Angie, two people for whom I had great respect. God had used them as instruments to help me come across to God. I was excited about telling them, thinking that they would be pleased for me. I invited them to a restaurant for breakfast and told them that Mike and I were going to be betrothed. The only way I can say it was they went into shock! To them, it was the worst thing I could do. They told me that Mike was not the right man for me and that it would ruin my walk with the Lord. They said to me, "Be careful, the enemy can easily get you back." They then went on and spoke to me like I was some fifteen years old, and they assumed that I was marry-ing Mike for sex." They told me that my flesh was weak. I walked out of the restaurant shocked, dazed, and confused. I had wanted their support badly.

I then went over the words that God Himself had given me and what He wanted for me. I was a real mess. No, I said to myself, God was so clear and real to me that day about marrying Mike. I was going to do what God wanted regardless of what other people were saying. I knew that Arthur and Angie meant well, but I didn't know where they were coming from at this point. I then informed another pastor and his wife, whom I was close with. Here comes another shocker. The wife said, "If you did this, I would go back with the devil." That did it! I put a wall up between them (and everyone else) and me. It was the only way I could survive. It was the only way I could deal with it, plus I kept screaming out to my Father that I was hurt by what these people had said, and I wanted to hurt them back. I screamed to God, "Help me, Lord!" I was so shocked and couldn't understand why they thought of Mike as garbage, and I was some brainless blonde. Neither couple even hesitated in coming forward with their negative statements. Again, why didn't they check in with the Holy Spirit for discernment about this whole situation? He would have told them the truth. In my mind, people were operating from their own feelings and beliefs.

I thought that when I told them that it was God that wanted us to be betrothed, I honestly thought that they would understand. None of them were listening. Why didn't they check in with the Holy Spirit? *He would have told them the truth.* How many times do people not listen to Him because they have prejudice and preconceived ideas about another person. So, as a result, they are not able to hear what God is saying through it all, and they don't ask Him because they are so caught up in their own judgments. They have judged, so the verdict is out, and then they close the door in your face. If they had truly prayed to God, the truth would have been told.

At the same time, I was part of a pageant. It was a Victorian era pageant. We ladies were all dressed up in crinoline dresses. It was being held at the church I went to. It was wonderful. I had invited Mike to come along. That was not going to turn out quite so wonderful. My close friends at the church would speak to me, but they totally ignored Michael; in fact, only one lady actually spoke to him. A surge of anger rose up within me. *Okay, people*, I thought, *you would not check it out with God, and I can't do anything about that. If you do not accept Michael, then you do not accept me. God is putting us together, so I felt that my friends should get with the program.*

Even putting other people's thoughts aside, I was really struggling for three days about this whole thing betrothal to Michael and the warnings from people I had come to love. It almost felt like that every hour I was asking myself, "Should I or should I not become betrothed?" even though I had heard God's voice telling me that this was what He wanted for me. Then on the third day, I made a decision, and I said, "Yes, I would do this." The basis was that if God (my Father) was saying that this is what He wanted for me, He was also going to fix me up, take away all the crap that I had inside of me against all male figures. I did not like men because the demons that I had had inside me were male figures. To me, the devil was male, my ex-husbands were male, and my father was also male. So many bad experiences with *men*. So, I said to God, "Okay, I am going to take a chance, and I will do this."

I then phoned Mike and said that I was in agreement with what God wanted for us. Three days later, I was meeting Mike in the evening at his townhouse for supper. I arrived a little early, and he was not home yet. He had gone to see our pastor to explain what was going on between God and ourselves. I let myself in, and then he arrived. One look at his face and I was not comfortable, here we go again. "What's going on?" I said. Mike replied, "I spoke to the pastor, and he said that along with other things, prophets don't marry older women. So, we had better take another look at the whole thing, and I think it is better that we call the whole thing off. I only want to do God's will."

That was the first time that I had heard of Michael being a prophet, and what did older women have to do with it, anyway? What a backlash! And here I had made up my mind finally and said, "Yes, I would go through with the marriage." Now Michael had changed his mind and said no based on what this pastor had said to him. I was stunned, confused, and unsteady in my mind. Spiritually, it brought me to my knees. How could they do this to me? Who are they—the Pastor, Mike, the devil, and God? Was I still a puppet? Waves of rejection and hurt swept over me. I think Mike was still talking and apologizing for the change in his heart. My reaction in my mind was, "What a chicken." I wondered why all of them seemed to be trying to wipe me from the face of the earth. I took several deep breaths. *Steady here. Think, Gloria!* It was torture! I knew demons had tormented me, but now this!

I said to myself, *You have been at rock bottom before, and you still survived. This too I will get over. Tomorrow is another day. This will not finish me.* Then I promptly turned on Mike and, in turn, turned on the pastor and then the devil and all of his helpers and lastly God. I called Mike and the pastor everything I could think of and more, with words I will not even write down. How long I yelled, screamed, and cried; I didn't know, but it made me feel a little better. I then said to Mike, "I'm going to Port Stanley. I won't see you later." On the beach at Port Stanley, it was a place I would go to get my peace back, sort myself out, steady my feet, and get my life back. Just before I left, I saw the look on Mike's face. I read his mind, and I said, "So, you think that because of you I am now going to commit suicide and wrap my car around a tree or something similar? Give me a break. None of you are worth that, and I will get over this!" I was infuriated with him.

Can you imagine the scene? Mike jumped into the car with me, uninvited. I called him everything all the way down to Port Stanley. I said what a chicken he was and told him what I thought of Christian men in general, past lives, present life, and everything else. As I pulled up into a parking spot overlooking the water, Mike was still in the car saying nothing. I started to feel the strong presence of the Holy Spirit (Mike told me afterwards he also felt His presence). I felt much calmer then due to the influence of the Holy Spirit. Silently, we walked the beach together. The Holy Spirit's presence was surrounding us both and getting stronger and stronger. It was as if time had stood still. And it was going to stand still until this matter between us was resolved God's way, not man's way and most definitely not the devil's; only God's way.

God wanted us betrothed at *all* cost. Suddenly, I had so much love in my heart for Mike and he for me. We just looked at each other and said to each other, "I love you." With what I had just been through, only God's presence could have done that. The Holy Spirit melted both of our hearts. We were now back in the car, and the air was so thick from the Holy Spirit's presence that I think it floated out in a fifty-mile radius around us. It was all love. The Holy Spirit's relationship with Mike and me was so intense. His deep affection for us both, His desire for our lives together were awesome. He was going to make it work.

It wasn't going to be easy, but God was arranging our betrothal and marriage. It really couldn't get much better than that. Just think, an arranged marriage by our Father God. All the other stuff that had happened was gone and was no longer important. Just for the record, I had to still work on forgiving Michael and the pastor, and I also still had to deal with rejection, bitterness, and forgiveness in other areas of my life. The only way to describe it was that it was all like a big onion, and each layer was being peeled off one layer at a time over and over again. With God's help, I came through, and I forgave them. Just think this fun was going on *before* we got married.

My marriage to Mike, gosh! How do I explain all of this? The first time I met Michael was the night I gave my testimony for the first time, one year to the day after my deliverance. We lived in different towns, had different friends, and went to different churches. It was a well-known fact that Mike still loved his wife, and he made every effort to get back with her and his kids. This made it safe for me to be acquainted with him. I really didn't like men but had no problem being pleasant with them. God showed me how shallow I was in this area of my life. I required deep healing where men were concerned, but it was not going to be an overnight fix. God was in control of all this, thank goodness.

Over the next months, Mike and I met at different church functions and through people we both knew. Looking back, it seems quite funny because God had already started putting the two of us together, neither of us realizing what God was up to. For me, the Lord was teaching me that I could be genuinely friendly with a man—no pretending, no falseness. We did not see a lot of each other; sometimes we would call each other, and sometimes we would not see each other for a couple of months at a time. Things started heating up at a later date.

Before Mike and I were married, and even after it was being confirmed by God that this was what He wanted for us both, so many of my friends were against the marriage, but many more people were for it. I really didn't want to get married again; Mike did but to a younger woman. We were not romantically in love, and we certainly didn't date. There was not any courtship before our marriage. There were quite a lot of heated discussions between us and misunderstandings.

In January 1995, I went shopping with my daughter; Mike was not on the scene yet. I bought a lovely two-piece laced outfit, and the color was cream. Being a little too fancy for everyday wear, I hung it at the back of my closet and forgot about it. Darice reminded me about this outfit when I was wondering later that year what I would wear to my wedding. The outfit was perfect, problem solved.

About a month before the marriage, I pulled the two-piece outfit out of my closet. As I was an agent for dry cleaning at the store, when the man came for a pickup, I placed the cream-colored two-piece outfit in his hands, telling him to be careful with it, as I was planning on getting married on June 15. Bless him, he said he would do it for free for me.

This was my third wedding. I was just thinking about everything one day and thought, *Lord, I have never been married in white. It would have been nice to be in white this time.* A week before the wedding, I checked the closet where my outfit should have been hanging, and it was not there. As I was getting agitated with my wedding approaching. I phoned the dry cleaning company, asking where my outfit was, and I was told that it was delivered a week ago. Then I looked through every single piece of dry cleaning. Oh my goodness! There it was, but instead of my outfit being cream, it was now white. The lace was beautiful and all white. My wish was granted, my Father was giving me away in white. It was amazing, but that was God.

Our wedding took place in June 1995, it was small with only seventeen people in attendance. For our wedding night, it was planned for us to stay in my trailer in a beautiful park in Guelph. This was a brand-new trailer and my second home to get away from the stress of the store. Mike and I were tired after the events of the wedding day, so instead, we decided to stay at Mike's house in London planning on going to Guelph the next day. We went to the bedroom and crashed, turned off the lights, and then we kept hearing mosquitoes buzzing around, so on went the light. Mike was trying to kill them, off went the light again. More noise, on went the light. In the left-hand corner of the room near the window in the bedroom, there was a steady stream of different kinds of insects climbing up from the floor to the ceiling and then disappearing; the mass was maybe 1.5 inches wide from floor to ceiling. We couldn't believe our eyes. Mike started swatting them, and I ran downstairs to the same corner, and there were no insects there. I then found bug spray and went back up to the bedroom where the insects were. We sprayed and then prayed and then put the lights out and crashed. Upon waking the next morning, there was not one insect in that room, dead or alive. The spray can was still there but now empty. I have no idea what that was all about, but nothing happened to us, so praise the Lord.

We arrived at the trailer park the next day. I was not in good form; I was feeling pressured, and I felt that I was under a spiritual attack, and I was getting very emotional. We parked the car and went into the trailer. I was not comfortable with Mike, my new husband, at all. He sat on the edge of the bed, and then I had a meltdown. I remember screaming at him, telling him that I was leaving, going for a drive, and that I would be back later. I picked the keys up, slammed the trailer door, slammed the car door, and drove off. *I am not going back until I feel better*, I said to myself. I stopped at a stop sign while still on park property, and I was about to make a right turn to go onto the highway when God spoke to me. "Gloria, you must go back."

"I'll go back when I am good and ready," was my reply.

"Gloria, listen to me, you are now under the covering of your husband. To go out on the highway like this, an accident could happen, so go back." I argued back and forth. It would have looked like I was talking to myself if anyone was looking out of their windows. In the end, God prevailed. "Okay, I'll go back," I said. I turned back to the trailer, slammed the car door, and saw Mike was still sitting where I had left him. Angrily, I said, "What did you say to God that He told me to come back?" Mike replied, "Gloria, I was praying for your safety as directed by God." It took me a long time to calm down. We worked through a mountain of things with God's help. Just think of a roller coaster with all its ups and downs. I just kept saying to myself that this too would pass, and eventually it did.

The reception for our marriage didn't happen until December 31, 1995, six months later. There were about seventy-five to eighty people there. God was all over it. One of the guests said that the Lord had asked her to sing for us. She sang "Amazing Grace," which is my favorite hymn. How did she know? I had no idea what a beautiful voice she had. People gave their testimonies about what God had done in their lives during this reception. Everything was beautiful, and the love of our Father was there, and He was well pleased.

I thought at the time that getting married would solve all my problems. Instead, I had so many struggles with *me* and *marriage*. The first three and a half years of marriage for me and for my poor husband were dynamite. The blowups were coming from me. I packed Mike's suitcase so many times I am embarrassed to admit it, but I asked myself, why would he want to stay with someone like me? I felt that it was better I end it rather than have him leave me. I didn't know which side of me was up or down. I was yelling at God, "I told you this wouldn't work!" I had such distorted views on marriage, and I didn't trust my husband. Did I submit? Maybe, but it never lasted long. I was highly strung, and my emotions were all over the place. I told myself that I was *not* the problem, that Mike was (how convenient). Thank goodness God was in our lives. I felt there were times that God was not listening to me and that He was definitely siding with Mike. Then slowly, very slowly, I was learning to honor God in this marriage, and I started to stabilize and change. Proverb 16:3 says, "Commit your work to the LORD, then your plans will succeed."

Again, when I complained to God, He would not listen to me. It was to be sorted between husband and wife. Mike hung on in there, even in our darkest moments. I asked Mike often, "Why do you stay?" His reply was always a firm "God has not told me to leave yet." I did not know the problems Mike was having at the time. I was too busy trying to figure myself out and the baggage I brought in from two failed marriages (not as a Christian). With God in the mix, Mike and I had our good times and our bad. I wanted sex, Mike would say he wanted intimacy. He wanted to keep his friends, I didn't want to see anybody. A great deal of people saw God working in our lives, and it was good to hear them telling us this. By my standards, nothing seemed to be working. I had a hard time respecting my husband, and I didn't trust God enough to pray properly about giving me wisdom and strength to humble myself and learn from God.

Slowly, Mike and I drew closer, Mike even worked with me in the store for the last five years we owned it. God was teaching us about working and living together. We were learning to forgive when nasty things happened and just get on with the relationship.

God kept on showing me things that offended Him in His church. This particular incident happened in one of the larger churches in London. It was a Sunday evening near Christmas. Mike and I went specifically for the worship, which this church was famous for. The place was packed, and to find a seat, we had to go upstairs, and there right in the front row were two seats that were vacant to the left of the altar.

What a wonderful view of the congregation below and the altar. Worship and praise was very powerful. Worship went on for at least thirty minutes. While worshiping my God, I always have my eyes closed and hands raised. God whispered in my ear, "Gloria, open your eyes." "Lord," I replied, "I am worshiping you." His answer was, "Open your eyes." Then just prior to this, the pastor had spoken briefly on how, after an altar call, the same people went up to the front of the church week after week, month after month, year after year, with no change, no good fruit showing. They needed to grow up and not remain stagnant, for Jesus stands for life, not death. He then proceeded to sprinkle holy water over the steps from one end of the altar to the other and also on the carpet near where the people were sitting. He sprinkled so much water I thought that the carpet was going to be really wet.

Back to the praise and worship. I had my eyes open, and at first, I saw nothing. Then coming out from under the canopy below came a line of demons; they were shoulder to shoulder, wall to wall, walking through the congregation, eyes straight ahead, not rushing but moving at a steady pace. They were walking right up to the front of the altar, walking over and on the holy water. When they reached the front, they turned around, looked at the congregation for about a minute, and then vanished. How can they walk on holy water I asked myself?

The Lord showed me that the church was spiraling down spiritually despite the prophecies that were being spoken out about it. "How many churches," the Lord asked me, "have gods in front of my altars?" Spiritually, I could see an Asherah pole in front of that church's altar. Not a good scene. The Lord had me intercede against these things in other churches in the past and in the spirit tear down and destroy the poles. What the Lord God had showed me in that church in London has stayed with me even up to today. 2 Kings 23:6 says, "The King removed the Asherahpole from the LORD's Temple and took it outside Jerusalem to the Kidron Valley, where he burned it. Then he ground the pole to dust and threw the dust in the public cemetery."

Mike and I were going out to go to a Bible study in London. It was a Wednesday, so it was an early closing at six in the evening. I looked out, and the snow was really coming down. A half hour later, it was even worse, so we decided to stay home and have a Bible study in the apartment. I had no idea what I was about to see.

Mike started to read 1 Peter 2:1 (LASB), "So get rid of all evil behavior. Be done with all deceit, hypocrisy, jealousy, and all unkind speech." I think we got to the word *hypocrisy*, and I was at this point still seated on the couch along with Mike. The room changed, and the floor in the middle of the room began to open up. Within the whole chasm itself, the hole was black. Instinctively, instead of looking down, I looked up. The demons were rolling in on black clouds, and there were flashes of lightning, and you could almost hear the thunder. There were many of them, and they were all looking at me. Oh, dear God, are they coming to get me?

I jumped up, all sorts of things crossing my mind at the same time. What had I done wrong to offend God, and why was this happening to me? I was sort of in survival mode. They were not going to take me over and possess me! Never again. Was I still an instrument, a mechanical robot that could still be controlled by them? They were not going to take me back—never—never! God, where are you? The hole in the floor was still widening, and more demons were still rolling in from the ceiling area above. What about my husband you may ask. Well, what about him? He was still sitting over on the couch where I had been sitting with him, Bible open, looking totally stunned. It was *me* who they were after—again! I was panic-stricken, and the fear from within me was mounting. Having stood up, I was banging my feet on the ground so I could feel the floor beneath me.

What I didn't like to see was that there were two of me. I cried out to God; I did not leave my body, and so why was I seeing two of me? I was seeing myself standing over the abyss, but the other half of me was jumping up and down on solid ground in the living room. Figure that one out, if you can. There were so many demons I could even smell them it was gross. Mike was still on the couch, and I was now on the other side of the room. I was agitated, angry, and hostile. For me, there appeared to be no escape. I called out, "Michael, grab my hand and help me!" There was absolutely no response from him. Again, I shouted, "I am in danger. You are doing nothing about this, help me and grab my hand!" "No," he said. Never, ever had I felt so vulnerable and alone. I exploded and called my husband every-thing, printable and unprintable, but still there was no change in him. Meanwhile, the demons were still pouring into the room. The black hole in the floor was getting bigger. I remember thinking that I am undone and ruined.

I remember challenging them, yelling at them, "You can take me, rip me apart, and swallow me, and I will give you such a case of indigestion you would have wished that you had not touched me, for I am a child of God." No, I was not laughing. Again I called to my husband, "Help me!" Still no response. It took at least two weeks after this incident to forgive Michael for not helping me, and after that, it took just as long to forgive my God. Abyss means a bottom-less pit. I myself stood right on the edge of that pit. But although I was drawn towards it, I was able to stand straight and not fall in. Then as suddenly as it had all began, it all disappeared. I was not in good shape, and immediately I verbally attacked my husband and my God. I challenged Mike and said, "You are such a chicken, why didn't you help me? God put us together. I demand that you give me an answer *now!*"

Well, first of all, he had not seen a thing. *I didn't believe him.* I thought any excuse is better than no excuse. I thought he was being cowardly. As I had explained before, it took two weeks to get over this incident, and I would not talk to him about it, as Michael tried to explain that Christ told him to *not* help me as Jesus Himself was with me. Again, I just didn't believe him, my God would not put me through something like that. He loved me. To cut a long story short, Jesus came to me one night in a vision. I was back in that living room, but this time, Jesus was holding me in the palm of His hand over the abyss, and nothing was going to come at me, and neither was I going down into that hellhole. And yes, He did speak to my husband and told him to not touch me, for I needed to see Him, Jesus. What can I say, I got over the incident (and myself), and I forgave where it was needed and went on with my life.

It was shortly after this that God gave me permission to go back to the earthworks and the dome. Mathew 6:9-15. (LASB) says,

> "Our Father in heaven, may your name be honored. May your Kingdom come soon. May your will be done here on earth, just as it is in heaven. Give us our food for today, and forgive us our sins, just as we have forgiven those who have sinned against us. And don't let us yield to temptation, but deliver us from the evil one."

> "If you forgive those who sin against you, your heavenly Father will forgive you. But if you refuse to forgive others, your Father will not forgive your sins."

This whole incident in our living room was created in preparation for me to go back to the earthworks and the dome. Because of my past, there was no doubt in my mind we were going to be under spiritual attack when there. But I really had to see that, and although there was danger all around me, I was really in no danger because Christ was in me. I had to be solid with that knowledge, I had to know that Jesus was protecting me, I had to have all other fear driven out of me, as I was still periodically fearing that the demons would take me back, so this was God and Jesus's way of conveying to me that I was safe. I needed to go to the earthworks and back to the dome with no fear.

Seven years had now passed since my deliverance. On the night, I had this dream, Jesus took me back to the prehistoric earthworks, showed me where I used to pray, where I had walked through the entrance that leads into the small maze, and from there into the spiritual center of the trees. Then He took me back to the dome. Everything was crystal clear. As my dream faded, I heard Jesus say, "My child, you have now revisited this place in the spiritual, and I was with you. Now it is time for you to go back in the flesh." I promptly woke up. I just knew that it was going to be exactly two weeks when Mike and I would visit both the earthworks and the dome in the flesh.

During this period, I had a hard time fighting to keep fear from invading my thoughts. With all the evil that was in these places, I felt that we were going to need an army of Christians praying for us. Also, we would need a CD player, so worship music could be played nonstop while we were there. And of course, our Bibles must come with us. My mind was in turmoil. (I then thought that it would not be right to put people in harm's way to pray against the evil that had been in my life. It could attack them, and even attach itself to them.)

I didn't want this on my conscience. I could be putting them in danger, both physically and spiritually. Many memories came back to me, none of them good. An understanding came within my spirit—I only needed Jesus to come with us and nothing else.

The day of our visit dawned. Jesus was with us. First, we went to the earth works. I knew instinctively where to pray, down I went on my knees, and then on my face, weeping and asking for forgiveness, and then I forgave myself. I thanked Jesus for coming into my life and bringing so much light and change—changes for the better.

Mike, in the meantime, was slowly walking the perimeter of the trees, praying, and sprinkling holy water on the ground. With my eyes closed, I saw in the spirit Mike as a red moving spot. The holy water was little drops of crystal white light. I could see the enemy coming against Mike in waves, their color a dark purple. Every time they came to attack us, Jesus's presence came between them and us, throwing the enemy back. Neither of us could be touched; God's love was all over us. Again and again, they came in waves, lunging at Mike, and every time Jesus came between them and us, throwing them back with amazing force. The earthworks was now spiritually cleansed.

Now onto the dome, which, of course, I did not own anymore. I did not want to go. Dumb though it may sound, going to get ice cream seemed a much better idea, and after what happened at the earthworks, ice cream was a really good idea. I just wanted to run away from all this "stuff." I didn't want to be ungrateful; I just wanted to be somewhat normal.

We arrived at the entrance to the dome property. Remember now my ex-husband had kept the dome in the divorce settlement (remember the battle in the lawyer's office). I saw a couple raking leaves, and they apparently now owned this place. I explained to them that my ex-husband and I had previously owned this property. I asked if they wouldn't mind if Mike and I looked around. They were right at home with us. God had gone before us, and the place was now ready to receive us with honor. We were told to go anywhere we wished, and they invited us to even look inside the dome. "Yes, yes, and yes," I said. It was the first time Mike had seen the dome. Trying not to show too much excitement, I wanted to see if the place was "spiritually" clean. We all walked together towards the dome. The couple seemed to know what they had to do and allowed us to enter every room and see every nook and cranny on each floor.

Look at the photo of the five-star window, way back when the spirits had me design the window, I felt uncomfortable and told them that I thought it evil. Over a period of three days, they convinced me all was well. The window was a good sign, *they* said (the spirits, not the people). Interesting! Yes? All this was already mentioned in the book. The window has two points upward, which is the sign of satan. The couple said that they were thinking of boarding the window up, which we agreed would be a great idea. God had done a marvelous job of cleansing the land and the dome already before I had even gone there. There was no unnatural heaviness, the birds were singing, and there was no sense of evil anywhere. All spiritual evil residents had perished at the hands of my Lord God. Restoration had come to the land and all who lived upon it. Everything was clean and pure spiritually and physically. What a day! And I too was clean. Praise you, Father. Praise you, Jesus. Praise you, Holy Spirit. I have not gone back since there is no need to. The number 7 is the sign of completion in the Christian faith. Meaning it has been seven years since I was allowed to go back and seven years since my deliverance. Father of my life, I will love You forever and ever.

Psalm 21: 8-9 says, "Your hand will lay hold on all your enemies; your right hand will seize your foes. At the time of your appearing you will make them like a fiery furnace. In his wrath the LORD will swallow them up, and his fire will consume them."

Psalm 119: 73-76: "You (God) made me; you created me. Now give me the sense to follow your commands. May all who fear you find in me a cause for joy, for I have put my hope in your word. I know, O LORD, that your decisions are fair; you disciplined me because I needed it. Now let your unfailing love comfort me, just as you promised me, your servant."

CHAPTER 24

Tested Again

Here comes another Thanksgiving. Mike and I had invited some friends to come to our apartment for supper. Although prior to my deliverance God had me destroy jewelry, artifacts, and clothing, He was now beginning to pressure me about nine gold rings, a gold necklace, and a gold watch that I had inherited from my grandmother and my mother. Not being one to wear rings, I hardly wore them. They were beautiful pieces but still from my family's unholy past. After being divorced from my first husband, I had given my daughter my gold wedding band and engagement ring her father had given to me, and strangely enough, two months later, they were both stolen from where she was living. Strange, I thought, but I also thought would anyone who knew my background really want to keep any jewelry of mine? Back to the nine rings and other jewelry, Michael didn't remember me showing them to him, but I had, and I was getting more and more pressure from the Lord to get rid of them. What I really wanted to do was to give them to my two children as gifts.

Really, could they harm my children? So, sounding really dumb as I think about it now, I said to God, would it be permissible to melt the pieces down and give the money to the poor? Who did I think

I was fooling here? God will not be fooled nor will He be mocked. The answer came back straight as an arrow right during this evening dinner with our friends. God said to me, "Do you love these pieces, or do you love Me?" This had been an ongoing concern of mine for a few weeks. I had a plan for the jewelry, and I wasn't hearing or accepting what God's plan was. Then in front of our guests, using them as witnesses, I brought the jewelry down; I took the pieces out back and smashed every piece of that jewelry with a sledgehammer with Mike helping me. Then all the fragments were put into a bag and then into another bag of garbage and spread the bits among different types of garbage to be collected for the dump by the garbage men. That jewelry was not good for my children or to be sold. Who knows what would have happened to the people who bought them? I knew our guests must have thought I was slightly impaired. No! I just had a past that nobody needed to be touched by. How great is our God. It seemed to be important to do this, all in front of our friends, as they acted as witnesses to this purging and destruction of the jewelry as led by the Lord. He was destroying my evil past and leaving no stone unturned to do so.

In 1 Corinthians 10:20–24 (LASB), it says,

> "No, not at all. What I am saying is that these sacrifices are offered to demons, not to God. And I don't want any of you to be partners with demons. You cannot drink from the cup of the LORD and from the cup of demons, too. You can not eat at the Lord's Table and at the table of demons, too. What? Do you dare to rouse the Lord's jealousy as Israel did? Do you think we are stronger than he is? You say, "I am allowed to do anything" – but not everything is helpful. You say, "I am allowed to do anything" – but not everything is beneficial. Don't think only of your own good. Think of other Christians and what is best for them."

So, here is a question for you: whose cup do *you* drink from, God's or satan's? Remember there are only two choices!

At yet another church we were visiting, this was an evening service. We knew the pastor and his wife quite well because of our involvement with The March for Jesus. Once again, I was worshiping the Lord with my eyes closed when Mike gave me a gentle nudge. He said, "The pastor's wife wants to see you." I looked over to the other side of the church. She was sitting next to a young woman who, I could see, had demons in her. The pastor and his wife were bound and bent that this woman would be delivered and set free that very night.

I was asked to help because of my background. We were all praying around her, and nothing was happening. My husband said to me, "Gloria, she doesn't want to let the demons go. Let her be." I wasn't getting that same information; in fact, I wasn't getting anything. Now I am on my face, still praying and interceding, and I see this albino snake slithering away. *Shelve that, Gloria*, I said to myself. The pastor by this time had gone and gotten a book on deliverance from his office and was waving it over the woman's head. But nothing was happening. Mike asked the woman, "Do you want to be set free?" "No," she replied. As she said no, I saw another larger albino snake slithering away and just knew it had bitten someone who had been around this woman. I saw it, and then I forgot all about the snakes.

Nothing happened with the woman. If a person doesn't want to give up their demons, nothing will get rid of them. All the excitement went down to a dull roar. I was upset because I had not wanted to go over and minister to her in the first place. Mike and I talked about it all and then just dropped it. All this happened on a Sunday night. Now it was Monday morning, and I was in the bathroom getting ready to go out. The Lord spoke to me. "Gloria, what did you see last night?" I immediately remembered the snakes. "Lord, there were two snakes." And the Lord replied, "Correct." I said, "One had left, and then the second one had bitten somebody." "Who did it bite?" asked the Lord. Oh, horrors upon horrors, I realized that it had bitten *me*!

Shaking and scared, I cried out, "Help me, God, against that foul poison that is now in my body." I thought I was done, finished, and spiritually dead because of that thing that had the right to bite me. God gently spoke to me. "Did I give you permission to minister to that woman? And did you ask me for permission to minister to that woman?" "No, Lord," I replied. "So, why did you put yourself in harm's way?" He answered. Then I started to say, "Well, it wasn't my fault. My husband had nudged me, and I was being obedient to the pastor and his wife." God would have none of this. Obedience to Him first, not as I think.

The poison within me God had counteracted, and He warned me to not let this happen again. That whole incident was freaky. I didn't think it was fair, but I understood why God did what He did. God was looking after me, and this was part of my training. Maybe not normal to you reading this but quite normal to me. And I want to live and tell the things that God has done in my life to people who are as weird as I am. Praise the Lord, oh my soul, and all that is within me. Praise His holy name!

CHAPTER 25

Very Slow Learner

Over the next few years, I was still being transformed and still married to Mike. We were out buying for the store, and again it was Halloween. I spotted these two gargoyles, you know, the ones that are on old Cathedrals and churches in Europe put there to ward off evil spirits and demons. What a joke, that is just a huge welcome sign. By the way, do you have any of these creatures in your house or garden? These gargoyles were door stops—open the door and they scream at you. Mike asked me why I was buying them, and my reply was, "Because I want to." Just think how disgusting that was with all that my God had done for me.

Well, I was in for a shock, and it serves me right. Three or four days later, we came home late. The store was closed, so when we unlocked the front door, I thought all the demons in hell were not just screaming at me but also actually screeching at me. The noise was deafening. My self-righteousness about buying the gargoyles went from a high of ten to minus ten in one second. What happened? The girls at the store for a joke had put one of the ugly creatures on the door, so it would scream as the door opened, but it was not the only thing screeching. I learned a big lesson that night—I cannot play, or even think I can play, around with these things. How dare I dishonor

God and Jesus like this. I knew better, but I still went ahead and bought them, I can't blame the devil for this one; it was all my fault. I asked God to forgive me, and I took them back to the suppliers. Mike knew I should not have bought them, and he prayed to God about it. I wouldn't listen to him or God.

Now we were going to a gift show in Toronto. We had discussed how much money was to be spent at this specific gift show. When we arrived, we wore our badges, and everything was going smoothly until we reached a certain booth. The giftware was extremely good with amazing prices and "specials." With one of the salespersons, I started to give my order. Then the old self started to rise up within me, I just kept on ordering. At one point, Mike came over to me and said, "I think we have ordered enough," reminding me of our agreement of how much we were going to spend. I was not interested in hearing this, as I was now on a roll with my order. Mike interrupted again and said, "If you keep this up, I am leaving." "Good," I said, "I'll find my own way home."

The salesperson was very uncomfortable, so I told her to just get on with her work. I then finished giving the order and walked away from the booth. Then I saw my husband standing in the aisle, and as you can imagine, he was not happy with me. I felt fine. He was the one with the problem, not me. Not speaking, we started to walk around when suddenly, right in front of me, Jesus appeared, and He was about eight feet tall. "Gloria," He said to me, "why do you do this to me?" I honestly thought that everybody in that place must have seen and heard Him. He then said, "This is not my way. Ask for my forgiveness, and when this has been done, go ask your husband to forgive you." What? I thought. I was definitely stopped in my tracks, and I knew I was at a cross roads again. My mind was reeling, were people watching? What were they seeing? How long it took, I don't know.

(1) I asked my Lord Jesus to forgive my actions. (2) Then when Mike and I found a coffee area, we sat down, and I asked him to forgive me. He then told me how he felt about the incident, and I had to sit and listen. What could I say? I was speechless, I just listened to him express his feelings. Mike had not seen Jesus, but he knew some-

thing was happening to me. (3) I did not go back to see the salesclerk to apologize for my disgusting behavior, but I know now I should have. We left the show early and took time out for ourselves (Jesus in the center). This incident reminded me of Paul who was Saul in Acts 9:3-9 while on the road to Damascus. As he (Saul/Paul) was approaching Damascus on this mission (he was persecuting anybody who believed in Jesus Christ), a light from heaven suddenly shone down around him. He fell to the ground and heard a voice saying to him, "Saul! Saul! Why are you persecuting me?" "Who are you, Lord?" Saul asked. And the voice replied, "I am Jesus, the one you are persecuting!"…Nobody who was with Paul saw anything, but they knew something was happening. As Paul was stopped in his tracks, so was I at the gift show, the difference being that I could still see and Paul was sightless for three days. God's grace is amazing!

Mike and I still had the store, but we knew God was at long last moving us on to other things. Then God gave Mike a scripture from Deuteronomy that indicated we were to go north. Mike asked me to read the scripture one Friday morning, but at that particular moment, it didn't do anything for me. A couple of days later on Monday morning, God instructed me to read it again—yes, we were to go north. Now I am in total agreement about going north, but how far north and what city? We didn't have a clue. I guess the time was not right for us to know. Jokingly, we thought North Bay, Sudbury, or Timmins. I don't like the cold, and up there it would be very cold.

On our days off, at the store, we started driving north. We looked at some houses in Goderich to buy, but nothing ever materialized there. We even stayed at a B&B in Goderich, and it was a nice place, and amazingly it happened to be for sale. We asked the Lord whether this was the place or not. We both sensed that it was not. Then we went onto Kincardine, Port Elgin, and Southampton and then back to Kincardine. It was in Kincardine that we bought a lovely Cape Cod designed house. The plan was that I would run a B&B here when the store sold, and this was as far north as I was happy to go. It was great to have a house; I had not owned a house in over twenty-two years.

The house was ours; we couldn't believe all that was happening. Then I was starting to get worried and anxious about whether this really was the right thing to do, to buy a house and be a home owner and not a business owner. I was actually starting to have a life with a husband, and we ran a B&B. This new life was all very simple and humble compared to the life I lived at the store. I started pestering my Father (God), asking, "Is this for real? Is this the right place? Did we do this right?" and on and on like that. Then God gave me a vision. I was lifted up, looking down on the house; it was a bird's-eye view. Then suddenly, an arm came out of the heavens and out of the clouds. There was a signet ring on one of his fingers. The signet ring came right down upon the house. "There, my child," God said. "Now do you believe?"

"I do believe, but help me overcome my unbelief!" (Mark 9:24, LASB).

I was learning that growing in faith is a constant process. It is a daily task. I had so much to learn still. Thank you, God, for how you are towards me. This was the house that God had decreed was *ours*!

Mike went out to work, and I ran the B&B, and I loved it. Later we bought the land next to our house, and we started to build another B&B. Things, for one reason or another, went sadly wrong with this whole project. This went on for about two and a half years. We nearly went broke. People were amazed we stayed together through this. It wasn't a problem staying together; it was what was happening to our finances, and it seemed that everything we touched went wrong. Again, thank you, God, that you were in our lives. Ecclesiastes 4:12 says, "A person standing alone can be attacked and defeated, but two can stand back-to-back and conquer. Three are even better, for a triple-braided cord is not easily broken."

It was during this period that I told people not to call me a Christian. Why? Because I would have been a hypocrite; I was just plain nasty. We nearly went bankrupt, but God came to our rescue here again. We were able to rent the house out for two years for an unbelievable monthly rent. Only the Lord could have done that! The new house we had built stayed in our possession for seven years. After we sold it, we moved to a village near The Blue Mountains in Ontario. Mike got a job with a large company as a flooring contractor. We worked together, sometimes with helpers if needed. It was hard work, but God was our boss, and we recouped a lot of our finances that the enemy had stolen.

CONCLUSION

As the years passed by, there have been amazing differences in my life. God has revealed Himself to me to be the Father I've always wanted. I can talk to Him about anything. How precious are your thoughts about me, O God. They cannot be numbered. I cannot even count them. They outnumber the grains of sand! And when I awake, You are still with me. Father, I adore You! No one can take Your place in my life. I pray that You are pleased with the Book, which would never have been written had You not come into my life. I pray that others such as I was would read this manuscript and come to know You as deeply as I have. Thank You for staying with me and making sure I have a real relationship with You before You sent me back into the world, a new creation in Christ. I want to be everything You created me to be. Thank You for changing my life. Everything I have comes from You.

Now you have read what God is doing in my life, why not go one step further and pray the prayer below out loud. Believe as you speak it. God will hear 'every' word you say:

"Lord Jesus, I believe you are the Son of God and as John 14 : 6 says, "I (Jesus) am the way, the truth and the life. No one can come to the Father (God) except through Me." All I am is yours Jesus. Forgive my pride, ego, self-righteousness and self-dependence. I confess all my sins to you, which are… I repent of all my sins and make you Jesus-LORD in every area of my life. I freely forgive all who have wronged me. I break any and all contracts I have made knowingly or unknowingly concerning the occult, false religions, and all other things You God loathe and detest. Lord Jesus, thank you that you died for me so I will be redeemed from every curse placed against me in my life. Dear God, let your presence come into my life so I may receive the deliverance I have need of. I bow my knee only to You Father, Jesus and the Holy Spirit. With You within me I can resist the enemy of my soul, satan. Amen and Amen.

Read Colossians 2:13-15......Then God made you alive with Christ. He forgave all our sins. He cancelled the record that contained the charges against us. He took it and destroyed it be nailing it to Christ's cross. In this way, God disarmed the evil rulers and authorities. He shamed them publicly by his victory over them on the cross of Jesus.

"Come, Lord Jesus, Come."

You can contact Gloria and
found out more about her life
and testimony by email at
mikeandgloriamurphy@gmail.com

ABOUT THE AUTHOR

Was born in England, December 9th. 1938. Immigrated to Canada when I was 23 years old. The first 50 years of my life consisted of being guided and trained by Spiritual Entities. Under their direction I was building a geometric dome, (or round house) for end times. Spiritual Beings were teaching me. Spent time in a Psychiatric Hospital. Had on going psychiatric help for 8 years. Have worked all my life, it helped to keep me sane. Have 2 children a girl and boy. Was delivered (rescued) at the age of 50. The curse that had run through the female line for generations was broken. Through the Grace of God my life has become completely turned around in ways I could never have imagined.

CPSIA information can be obtained
at www.ICGtesting.com
Printed in the USA
LVHW07s2030070818
586301LV00011B/22/P